The BUGEATER LUNCH and SUPPER CLUB

Endorsements

"I've known Mike Gleeson as the greatest Nebraska fan in the world. Not the richest, that's Warren Buffet. I had no idea Mike was in the mortgage business. I had no idea he ever had a job. I can't wait to read about it."
—**Tony Kornheiser**, Co-host of *Pardon the Interruption* on ESPN since 2001, Host of the Tony Kornheiser Show, ESPN Analyst and Commentator

"No matter what game you play, this book will show you how the game is played! Lessons learned from these mortgage "professionals" can be applied to life, love, or business! If you have a sense of humor and want a better understanding of human behavior, the *Bugeater Lunch and Supper Club* will laugh you in the right direction!"
—**Bradley T. Bleasdale,** Former Financial Advisor, currently the largest raw goat milk producer in Tennessee

"I enjoyed the book; this is an accurate recap of the heady sales culture in the mortgage industry during the period. I personally know Eddie and I knew Daddy. They are legends in the business. This is a great read for anyone who has ever bought a home."
—**Sean Higgins,** Industry Insider

"Well, he finally did it! I met Mike Gleeson in 1968 when we began our freshman year at Regis College in Denver Colorado. For the next four years and the following 50, Mike has been embellishing stories with me about everything from family, religion, politics, friends, celebrities, Nebraska football, jokes, his excellent golf game and, of course, the Mortgage Banking Business.

"For over 50 years I've been telling Mike, "You need to write a book." He actually followed my advice and teamed up with a couple of characters to write, THE BUGEATER LUNCH AND SUPPER CLUB. If you are looking for some laughs and may actually learn something, this book is for you."
—**Dave Nichols**, CEO High Country Beverage

"As a former Comic MC and behind the scenes veteran of the country music entertainment industry where I've seen it all, I can tell you the characters and stories in this book take the cake. If you're looking for lots of laughs, this book will not disappoint."
—**Rod Harris,** Artist Manager and Former President of Nashville Association of Talent Directors

"I went to college with Mike. Everyone had a nickname. He was called the Bar Czar because he managed the on-campus bar. The nicknames continued into his business career. Every character in the books has a nickname. Eddie the Pec, Daddy, Wall Street Joe, Big Marvin, etc. The behind-the-scenes shenanigans are hilarious. If you loved the Wolf of Wall Street, you'll love this book."
—**Frank "Rip" Fernholz** Regis University class of 1972 – Retired

"Some books knock you out of your chair, laughing so hard you can't breathe. Others knock you out of your chair with sheer astonishment. *The Bugeater Lunch and Supper Club*, amazingly, does both. Sharply written, but never taking itself or its cast of characters too seriously, this book is simply a joy to read. Had I only known then, what I know now about the sausage factory called "mortgage banking", I would have quit law and jumped right in. An absolute riot!"
—**John Mueller, B.A., J.D.**

"I met Mike Gleeson in 1968 as a Freshman at Regis College in Denver, Colorado and was reacquainted at our numerous and memorable reunions over the last 50 years. He always had the great stories and hilarious antics about his life, work and of course, golf. He has managed to put all this in an entertaining and informative book,

Bugeaters Lunch and Supper Club. It is a laugh out loud pleasure to read! Enjoy!"
—**Sandy Sollitt Noonan**, friend, classmate and fan

"*The BUGEATER LUNCH AND SUPPER CLUB* brought back many fine memories of mine, when I was a loan originator in Long Beach, CA during the early 1990's. I was an airline pilot and was recruited by a Mortgage Banker friend who told me I could make some extra money on my days off. It was a fast and furious time in Mortgage Banking. I got caught up in the zany life that Daddy in the *Bugeater Lunch and Supper Club* depicts in all its splendor, excitement, humor and fast pace. This book is a look into those times and how a large number of people were helped with home ownership by a bunch of individuals from all kinds of backgrounds and experiences and not a lot of mortgage business knowledge. A fun read with very entertaining accounts of those magical days."
—**J. Marty Noonan**, USAF Pilot, Retired Airline Captain, Ex-Part Time Loan Originator

"*The Bugeater Lunch & Supper Club* offers insight into the Mortgage Banking Industry that makes even the Irish blush. The fun of it all is the humor, friendships and gags the author shares makes it a great read. Mike Gleeson came from a wonderful O'Neill Nebraska family. He is a legend in our part of the world as a local boy who "done good," and made us proud.

I met Mike when he was an aspiring law student… and I was Nebraska's Director of Motors Vehicles & Hwy Safety. If you want an insightful, interesting and fun read…this one will fill the bill for you."
—**John L Sullivan**, Lincoln, NE

"I've had the pleasure of knowing Mike Gleeson for over 55 years. We had a lot of fun attending college together, but more importantly, as difficult as it's been, we've always shared the love of the Nebraska Cornhuskers football team… the original *Bugeaters*!!! You guys have accomplished something I never thought possible — you wrote and published a book about an industry and its cast of characters that most don't have a clue about, but you've done it in a way that people really enjoy reading the book.

Well done!! Mike (Eddie the Pec), your ability to write *The Bugeater Lunch and Supper Club,* is proof that at least one of us was paying attention during classes at Regis. Congratulations and best wishes with your book! It's a book everyone will enjoy."
—**Kevin "Bugs" Moran**, Omaha, NE

"WOW! Finally a book about the mortgage loan industry that honestly "tells it like it is!!!" I was a mortgage loan officer for over 15 years and Mike definitely "nails it" when discussing the characters in his book. We all had our "Daddy's" and L.O.'s such as Eddie the Pec and Johnny Gumbaz that we worked with… and all from such diverse backgrounds that it was amazing that we managed to close loans, make money, and stay out of trouble. This book is a great read for anyone in the industry… along with those who may be applying for a loan or have gone through the process. The book made me laugh and rekindled many fond memories of the mortgage business. I recommend *The Bugeater Lunch and Supper Club* and congratulate Mike on a funny and enjoyable read."
—**Jim Daopoulos**, Retired National Football Official, Retired Mortgage Loan Officer

"You don't need to be an expert in the world of mortgage banking, or consider yourself a sports aficionado to appreciate and enjoy the writings of Mike Gleeson and friends. Connecting the two subjects would seem unusual but Mike does so flawlessly and with addicting entertainment value. An extremely enlightening read."
—**Steve Buckhantz**, Sportscaster

"Reading this book cast my memory back nearly thirty years ago when I initially heard these wild and wonderful stories told first-hand by the inimitable author, Michael Gleeson. I was a new rep, in a new business, in a new territory, calling on these crazy offices and leave it

up to Michael to strike up a new friendship with someone he barely knew—someone yearning to belong, who appreciates a good story. And who doesn't, right? This book, like Michael himself, has a way of holding you captive and leaving you wanting to hear more. Set in the less-than-sexy backdrop of mortgage banking, these comical stories pop off the page in vivid colors painted by the equally colorful characters regaling them. Michael Gleeson's entertaining encounter with Washington Post's/ESPN's Michael Wilbon remains one of my all-time personal favorites to this day."
—**Milan Kosanovich**, (Harvard Grad &) Certified Mortgage Banker

"In my twenty-five plus years in the mortgage banking business, I can attest to these shenanigans. The loan officers, processors, underwriters, and CEOs described within are real. I met a few of them. The authors have left no details out when describing this exciting and insane world of the past. This humorous and behind the scenes book is well worth the read."
—**Jeffrey Phillips**, Mortgage Banking Software Developer

The BUGEATER LUNCH and SUPPER CLUB

If They Only Knew... The True Comedic Inside Story of the Mortgage Banking Industry in its Glory Days

RICK SOPER,
MIKE GLEESON, DAVID RIDDLE

Goodyear, Arizona

Copyright 2024 by Rick Soper, Mike Gleeson, David Riddle, and Chuck Cepak
The Bugeater Lunch and Supper Club
If they Only Knew... The True Comedic Inside Story of the Mortgage Banking Industry in its Glory Days

eBook ISBN: 978-1-962570-41-1
Paperback ISBN: 978-1-962570-42-8
Hardcover ISBN: 978-1-962570-43-5
Ingram Spark ISBN: 978-1-962570-44-2
Library of Congress Control Number: 2024903036

All rights reserved. Printed in the United States of America. No part of this book may be used or reproduced in any written form or by electronic or mechanical means, including information storage and retrieval systems, without written permission from the author, except for the use of brief quotations in a book review.

First published in the USA in 2024 by Rick Soper, Mike Gleeson, David Riddle, and Chuck Cepak

Publishing House: Spotlight Publishing House™ in Goodyear, AZ
Chief Editor: Lynn Thompson, Living on Purpose Communications
Contributing Editor: Charlotte Quinn, Mighty Quinn Productions
Book Cover: Laura Ricci
Executive Producer: Chuck Cepak
Mighty Quinn logo artist: Anthony Azzi

For information, contact: Charlotte Quinn
Mighty Quinn Productions
CQ@mightyquinn.tv

To Daddy
Who lived his life to the fullest,
and made it possible for many others to do so.

To Mr. Miller
one of the three original Bugeaters and Treasurer
whose spirit and humor provided a foundation
for the Bugeater Lunch and Supper Club.

To Dan Schmidt
a favorite son of Nebraska and Hall of Fame member
who endorsed and loved the Bugeater way of life.

May all Rest In Peace

Contents

Foreword xv
Introduction xix

1. Daddy 1
2. The Bugeater Lunch and Supper Club 7
3. What's in a Name? 19
4. Wilbon 25
5. Johnny Gumba 39
6. The Clown Prince of Mortgage Banking 47
7. Bow's Lackey 59
8. The Whipping Boy 69
9. Riding the Gravy Train 77
10. Realtors (or Pigeons in the Park?) 87
11. Loan Applicants or Victims? 101
12. The Journey 111
13. An Equal Opportunity Membership 127
14. Underwriters aka The Wizard of Oz? 139
15. The Drawer: Mini-Marketeers and Pocket Locks ... 153
16. The Company: A Human Resources Nightmare ... 163
17. An Air of Flatulence 173
18. Saturday Night Live Mortgage 181
19. Mortgage Banker of the Year 193

Acknowledgments 211
Author Biographies 213

Foreword

Players and coaches, call 'em all Ballers, think they're the only competitive SOBs in the whole wide world—until they're finished in the athletic arena and suddenly confront men and women who are sometimes just as obsessively competitive as they are, if more so. Then, in gen pop, they're introduced to salesmen and techies, science wonks, artists, and, well, bankers.

And that's where this story begins, more or less, with a banker as competitive as they get and a writer hellbent on always having the last word, a football team and mortgages and temporarily hurt feelings and, ultimately a long, dear friendship. And yes, a book. Not that it was written by the writer; it wasn't. It's the banker's book, the Bugeater.

How we got to this point of me even writing the Foreword is probably a story worth telling, a necessary flashback to the early 1990s, at least ten years before daily television, to my days of writing a sports column for *The Washington Post*. The topic one day was Nebraska football, and for whatever reason, I took off on the Cornhuskers and everything Big Red. Everything. I'd been to Lincoln on gamedays a few times and it's really a wonder to experience. I don't have any idea all these years later what triggered it. They'd call it "a hot take" now; then, it was a rant or simply the opinion of someone who'd covered college football for years. Maybe there was a measure of jealousy, having attended school—Northwestern—where football between 1940 and 1995 barely registered. But I doubt it. Hell, every single column on college football would have been rooted in envy.

Anyway, I'd already been a columnist for a half-dozen years by then, had already spent more than a dozen years around college football, so, it wasn't difficult to know who the greatest fanatics were and how deeply offended they all are, regardless of institution, when facing even the most benign public criticism. I knew—you can't write a credible column and not know—but didn't give a damn.

These, remember, were the days before social media, even before on-screen comments. When you wanted a piece of somebody, you found a phone number, dialed up the offending party, and verbally confronted 'em or left a nasty voicemail message with, of course, a return number. And Mike Gleeson, Nebraska's own, grandson of a Bugeater, did just that, probably while trying to finish his morning coffee with newspaper still in hand.

And the columnist, born and raised on the south side of Chicago and fancying himself a fairly tough guy, wasn't about to take the nasty voicemail message without a response. So, the banker got an equally and aggressively nasty voicemail in return! Fast forward to a Thursday or Friday months later, on a flight from Washington, D.C., where we both lived and worked, to Lincoln, Nebraska, and damn if Gleeson and I weren't on the same aircraft! I was headed out to cover the Nebraska-Colorado game, and Gleeson was en route to spending the Saturday being the dutiful Cornhusker he'd been all his life.

As usually happens with these things, ill-will gave way to polite hellos, then laughs, then a cordial breakfast in Chicago during the requisite 1990s layover at O'Hare. It wasn't exactly shocking that I'd become Public Enemy #1 throughout Nebraska. And nobody screaming on the local radio shows there would have any idea that Gleeson and I would go from screaming at each other on voicemails to playing dozens of rounds of golf together, being directly involved with encouraging each other's sons (only children, no less) throughout childhood, and doing a considerable amount of business together. No home purchased by me and my wife has been mortgaged by anybody not named Gleeson. Even competitive lunatics can apparently find common ground!

I told Gleeson, on the golf course, of course, that he wouldn't dare devote a chapter of his promised book to this insanity, which he vowed he would and did. The most fascinating stuff, by far, however, involves luncheons and day drinking and "Daddy" and the business of business. Specifically, mortgage banking. And to borrow a line from Gleeson's text that is dead-on true, readers will find these stories "enlightening, bewildering, hilarious, refreshingly honest, and—oh yes—scary."

It's all so relatable. Looks behind the curtain generally are, especially when the teller knows a good story or two—or twenty. The Bugeater Lunch and Supper Club is a glide through the industry, yes, but also through a culture as competitive as any. That I got to have a front-row seat to the telling is both a hoot and an honor!

—**Michael Wilbon**, Co-host of *Pardon the Interruption* on ESPN since 2001 and ESPN Analyst and Commentator

Introduction

Per Eddie the Pec:

In the summer of 1964, I accompanied my father to the local bank in O'Neill, Nebraska, to apply for a Veteran's Administration loan to purchase our new home. He took me along to get a taste of how the process worked.

We met with an older gentleman, a typical small-town stuffed-shirt banker, who had written the contract just that afternoon. My father planned to go to settlement the next day. The banker reviewed the contract, pulled out three documents, and asked my father to sign them. He said the cashier's check for $10,000 would be ready for pickup that afternoon. We went to settlement the next morning and our family moved into the new home that afternoon. The rate on the 30-year mortgage was 3.0 percent, and the closing costs came to a grand total of $850 with no down payment.

Fast forward 30 years to the early 1990s, when mortgage lending had become an enormous business with many more hands involved. With homeownership THE American Dream, the Federal Government wanted to make it easier to qualify for a loan. So, the Feds lowered the standards, opening the floodgates. As a result, homeownership jumped to nearly 65 percent.

That increase in qualified home buyers introduced an entirely new dimension for loan companies and the type of individuals hired to conduct the influx of new business.

Introduction

In the prosperous Northern Virginia real estate market, the experienced president of a highly-respected mortgage company, No. 1 in the region, assembled a team of loan originators. These loan officers on the front lines generating loans for their company came from a wide range of backgrounds. Used-car salesmen, Certified Public Accountants (CPAs), bartenders, a former-but-not-disbarred lawyer, and even a tow truck driver: a cast of characters who held the future of many families in their hands.

Imagine the scenario of no background checks, no credit checks, and no licensing requirements for these loan officers facilitating a process that prospective homeowners, many of them first-time buyers, really had no clue about – a pretty scary thought. The CEO – "Daddy" – ran a tight ship. His goal was to make as many loans as he could, make as much money as possible, not break the law – and have a whole lot of fun.

Sometimes the fun superseded all of the other goals!

This story revolves around Daddy, the cast of characters he assembled, and how successful everyone was despite themselves.

The average homebuyer has no idea what goes on behind the scenes of the loan process. Sometimes, loans are not approved until the actual day of settlement, involving much drama, some incompetence, and a lot of paper. It always seemed to work out at the end; it was just the journey in question. Daddy often called the whole process a matter of herding a bunch of cats.

That this group – the "Cadillac of Mortgage Bankers" – became the highest-producing office in the DC metropolitan area defies all logic. So, forget about the textbook definitions of FHA, VA, conventional loans, Fannie Mae, Freddie Mac. You can throw out the book and just keep this one. Getting a home loan can be like assembling a rocket ship from a comic book to fly to the moon.

This book wipes the lipstick off the mortgage banking industry while answering the question borrowers wonder most about: Can I afford to buy a house? Readers will find these stories enlightening, bewildering, hilarious, refreshingly honest, and – oh, yes – scary. But, somehow, despite all the behind-the-scenes shenanigans, this group of misfits succeeded in helping many Americans realize the American Dream of homeownership. This book is about money, human nature, stress, losing your composure, anger, screaming, promises kept and broken, unreturned phone calls, and cartoon-to-potty humor – and ultimately, stories of success and the house you live in.

We bet you can relate.

Rick Soper
Mike Gleeson
David Riddle

Chapter 1

Daddy

Daddy was the most interesting man in mortgage banking. He always drank beer, and when he did, he drank Coors Light (pronounced Kurz Lahtt). He did not stay thirsty long. Neither did his friends. At five-foot-nine and a well-groomed 250 pounds, his nickname was appropriate. Daddy was a father figure to mortgage banking in metropolitan Washington, DC, and The Company, which he founded in 1985. Like the children of a beloved and respected patriarch, many of his employees stayed with him for more than four decades. This loyalty was highly unusual in a fast-buck industry like mortgage banking, where people would move at the drop of a hat for a signing bonus or another host of false promises. Loyalty was of utmost importance to Daddy. He was an extremely generous and caring individual. He did not suffer disloyalty well.

Like many great success stories in sports and business, Daddy hailed from small-town America. He came from Indiana, where high school basketball was king. In fact, he played with Rick Mount, the first high school athlete featured on the cover of *Sports Illustrated*. He received a scholarship to Purdue University for basketball and also played golf there during his freshman year. He then transferred to Indiana University, where he played golf and graduated in three years in 1970.

The US Navy beckoned, and Daddy came a calling. He was, in essence, a financial analyst stationed in Japan. However, this became the first stop on his road to fame and, more specifically, fortune. He had access to golf courses where he spent considerable time. As a scratch golfer, he was in a position to hustle many of his fellow officers. And hustle them, he did. He built up a sizable war chest from his winnings, which eventually assisted him in getting started in the mortgage business. Daddy was extremely competitive. Whatever he did had some stakes involved. Golf, tennis, cards, arm wrestling, business – it didn't matter. The people he engaged in these activities came to learn a hard lesson, which was basically, "We ain't finished till I got your money."

Daddy finished up his stint in the Navy and returned to Indiana, ready to take on the business world. He knew some folks in mortgage banking in the St. Louis area and decided to take a shot at it. His experience in financial analysis with the Navy, his overall competitiveness, and his understanding of what made people tick all served him well. Things went relatively well in St. Louis, but Daddy was always looking for a bigger challenge or a greener pasture to conquer. In the mid-'70s, Northern Virginia was a sleepy bedroom community west of Washington, DC. Daddy's crystal ball somehow saw the enormous growth potential lying there. He was astute at looking down the road and keeping one step ahead of his competitors. He rarely made a bad decision, and his assessment of the future Northern Virginia real estate market was on point. His career there would eventually extend to five decades, in which the area became a booming metropolis stretching from DC to the West Virginia border. He would get in on the front end and ride a soon-to-be booming economy and real estate market.

In 1982, Daddy hooked up with a mortgage banking outfit in Fairfax, Virginia. He was soon running things and turning some healthy profits. After approximately three years, he felt it was time to start his own gig. From that point on, you could hear Daddy coming. Two elements defined his career: He had to be the main man, and would not tolerate corporate nonsense and control.

He founded The Company in 1985, lining up several banks that he could sell loans to and a group of investors. Then he assembled a core support group and recruited several loan originators from around the area. A primary enticement to these people was the offer of builder business. In line with his view of the tremendous growth in housing soon to occur in metro DC, was his strategy to align himself with the key builders in the area. The game was straightforward. Daddy guaranteed the builders that the loans on their new homes would be approved if there were any possible way to do so. He also lined up construction money that allowed them to complete large subdivision projects. In turn, the builders would write into the real estate contracts with the buyers that they would pay a percentage of their closing costs if they used The Company for their loans — creating guaranteed business for The Company and any loan officers that Daddy assigned to new home projects. In addition, Daddy sought originators who could produce "spot" loans on existing homes where real estate agents generally referred the buyers. Daddy had also cultivated some good relationships in the real estate brokerage community. As questionable as the backgrounds of some of these loan originators might be, they were smart enough to know that Daddy was a winner and that builder business would nicely supplement what they already had going.

Eddie the Pec had heard about Daddy and The Company. Eddie originally learned to sell at Xerox, which had an excellent sales training program at the time. He knew some people in the burgeoning mortgage banking business who were making some good money and did not have to work awfully hard to do so. So, in September 1983, Eddie decided to take the plunge. Three companies and two years later, he found himself at Daddy's doorstep. He signed up, and, as they say, the rest is history. Eddie would go on to have a long and lucrative mortgage banking career that spanned many companies and personalities. To this day, if asked about Daddy, he has no hesitation. Eddie will tell you that, hands down, Daddy was the most brilliant and colorful individual to ever operate in the bizarre mortgage-lending industry.

Daddy had already assembled quite a gaggle of geese for loan originators. His theory was that if he put together and maintained a sound support staff, he could afford to take some chances with these characters floating around the Northern Virginia mortgage banking scene. A man's man, Daddy liked to surround himself with guys who liked the same things he did: sports, hunting, fishing, and drinking – not necessarily in that order. Eddie found himself surrounded by characters like Wall Street Joe, Big Marvin, Mookie, The Zealist, and Mr. Z, among others. Of course, Eddie was something else himself. He soon realized that the best way to ingratiate oneself with Daddy was to show up daily at his favorite watering hole mid-to-late afternoon, Daddy would hold court for hours on end, telling stories as his circle pounded them down. Thankfully, he was unaware of the source of the stamina for many of his subjects that kept them going into the wee hours of the morning, including lines of cocaine that they constantly ingested in the men's or ladies' rooms. They figured that as long as Daddy didn't find out, it was okay to get a bump when needed. The practice was rampant enough that The Company CFO eventually became known as Eskimo.

The Company was making money, and Daddy was known for his generosity when things were going well. He was fond of rewarding his favorite loan originators by sponsoring hunting and fishing trips. He had a connection on the Eastern Shore of Maryland to rent out a goose and duck hunting lodge. With his trusty driver, Andrew, at the wheel, they would fire up The Company limousine, and off they would go. These trips had a consistent theme: participants spent 99 percent of the time drinking and 1 percent hunting. This routine included legendary late-night card games that would not end until Daddy had his way. In all probability, some of the guys would lose on purpose, so they might steal a meager two hours of sleep before Daddy forced them to appear in a frozen duck blind.

One time, there was no sleep at all as the crew piled into the chauffeured limo and rolled out toward the blind, as drunk as a bunch of loons – no pun intended. They pulled up, barely able to see the blind out in the frozen marsh, all wondering the same thing; do we really have to do this? Just then, a pack of geese wandering by stopped and stared at the limo. Daddy rolled down his window and started blasting some caps. His boys quickly followed suit. They took down several geese, which they laid on top of the limo. The geese mixed in well with the myriad collection of whiskey bottles they had already placed there. It made for one hell of a photograph, which someone managed to take. A job well done. Each year's trip was basically more of the same. In fact, the participants were a bit fuzzy on what actually occurred and were not quite certain if they hunted at all. Not that it mattered. They were out of the office with Daddy, and the booze flowed. Life was good.

The highlight of every trip was the card games – specifically, liar's poker. The game got started early and ran into the wee hours of the morning. Four o'clock came, and even the more seasoned drinkers would be fading badly. One time, there was nearly $2,000 in the pot when Eddie decided to play his hole card. That was a dollar bill with eight 2s on it, which he had been waiting to spring on Daddy since he joined The Company. The hand went around, and Eddie called out. "Twelve 2s!" Daddy laughed and said in his distinctive grunt-like manner, "No way in hell! I'm calling your dead ass!" They laid 'em down, and sure enough, Eddie had won. Daddy was in shock. He grabbed all of the money and walked to the nearest window, pulled it open, and threw the mess of bills out into the wind and cold. He turned around and cried, "Have fun finding it. I'm gonna sack out."

Eddie walked into the office Monday morning to find a check for $2,000 on his desk. Daddy hated to lose, but he was inevitably a good sport and generous to a fault. Eddie knew he had just had his 15 minutes in the sun. It wasn't going to happen again.

One of the amazing things about Daddy was his ability to get so many things done in a relatively short workday – short because the daily goal was to get the crew to the gin mill of choice by mid-afternoon at the latest. Words poured out of his mouth like a machine gun: "Good deal! Good deal!" He could certainly juggle a bunch of balls at the same time. A typical morning could involve interviewing a potential new hire, signing off on a couple of marginal loans, soliciting a new builder, and putting out some fires at the closing table. Daddy knew the top priority for builders and realtors alike was getting the loan package to the closing table on time and done the right way. Come hell or high water, that was going to happen. And if it didn't, someone would pay the price. Daddy buttered his bread on both sides. Performance meant increased referrals and an enhanced reputation. It was always surprising that more people in the mortgage banking management community didn't get it like he did. Of course, that was a distinct competitive advantage that Daddy would push to the limit.

The Company's first three years in the business were good. And business was growing. The Northern Virginia real estate market was hot, and Daddy and his boys were rockin' and rollin'. Because the mortgage banking industry was still relatively new, it was not overly saturated with loan originators. Loan originators claimed they could march into real estate offices, and the realtors would beg them to finance their deals. They could cherry-pick the loans they wanted and get premium pricing to boot. Everyone was making money and living large. But in such a volatile industry, it was only a matter of time before the chickens came home to roost. And soon enough, they did.

Chapter 2

The Bugeater Lunch and Supper Club

The Bugeater Lunch and Supper Club was born in the summer of 1988. Earl had recently joined The Company at the suggestion of Mr. Miller, who had only been on board since March. Earl and Mr. Miller had worked together at another lender in 1987. Earl's first stab at mortgage banking was an exciting learning experience. Having spent eight years in the trade association business, Earl was ready for a change. Mortgage banking offers the opportunity to make significantly more money and, to a large degree, work for yourself. By and large, it is a one-hundred-percent-commissioned business for loan originators where you make your own hours.

Earl was a natural and soon became the aristocrat of mortgage banking. Tall and muscular, he drove a brand new 300Z Nissan. Every morning, Earl was the first one in the office. He and Johnny Gumba drank coffee and gossiped their ears off about what companies were going down, what loan programs to add to the arsenal, and most importantly, who was the hottest girl in the office. Suspenders adorned Earl's gray suit and white shirt, but the shirttail always hung out of his pants in the rear. His shoes were shiny black. Paint cans were stacked underneath his desk. A boom box blared from on top of his filing cabinet.

It was difficult getting "dirt" on Earl. He did everything right. Always there. Always getting his business to settlement on time. Never late to any important meeting. He was one of the big hitters, so he had the unusual relational support of every commissioned and salaried person in The Company. But – he was vulnerable. He had an Achilles heel, something that would never go away, a constant thorn in his side. It was Eddie the Pec. If Earl had customers waiting in the lobby, and someone found out before he did, Eddie got to work.

The loudspeaker would blare: "Earl, please come to the main showroom floor... Earl, you have customers waiting on the main showroom floor." Although Earl had a swagger that accentuated his physique as he walked, which meant very little to his fellow Bugeaters, Earl rarely dared to leave his office to visit a client in the reception area, knowing Eddie would be up to something. When he did venture out, being a true Italian-Irishman, Earl had more than his fair share of facial hues from red to orange, so if you have ever witnessed a great white shark attack, you can imagine the look on the customer's face. When Earl walked them back to his aristocratic lair, they would arrive to see all the paint cans stacked on top of each other on his desk, with country music blaring so loud that people on other floors of the building would call reception complaining, "Hey, aristocrat, turn that music down! Don't you have any manners?"

Eddie would have a smile as big as life itself on his face. Earl, however, would not.

More backstory on Earl. As noted, he started his first job in the mortgage business in September 1987, the same month he was married. The bad news was that he had a long commute his first month. The good news was that effective October 1, a new office was opening near his home. Training went well, and he relocated to the new office on schedule. It was time to start generating some loans so he could get paid.

Kaboom! Fast forward to the end of the month and the infamous stock market crash. The sky was falling – or at least, Earl thought so. Business came to an abrupt halt, curtailing the ability to make any money. To make matters worse, when management announced on October 31 that the new office was shutting down, it was back to the grueling commute. Earl wondered, who shuts down an office after one month? Welcome to the unpredictable world of mortgage banking.

Things got progressively worse as the winter months rolled in. Earl's present employer, in essence, pulled out of the market; their rates were so high they were non-competitive. The branch manager began to set up broker relationships with other banks to fund any loans they could originate. Mr. Miller, who served as a mentor of sorts to Earl, was getting very nervous. He had been around long enough to know the game, and it was not going in his favor. It might be time to make a move.

The spring housing market began in March, and Mr. Miller moved on to The Company. It had an excellent reputation for getting loans done on time and the right way. Daddy had put together a well-oiled machine, and it was starting to hum. Mr. Miller arranged an interview for Earl with the branch manager. It went well. The branch manager made Earl an offer, but he turned it down. Earl felt he had only been in the business a short time and wanted to avoid becoming known as somebody who jumped from company to company.

During the first week of June, Earl's branch manger called a meeting and announced, "The bank is pulling out of the Northern Virginia market." He added that everything would turn out great, however, because some other bank would certainly come in soon and buy the branch. Earl had heard enough. He called The Company branch manager to explain the situation and to request another interview, which set up a meeting with Daddy.

Daddy was in an aggressive recruiting mode. He wanted to swell the originator ranks and ratchet up the volume. Earl was pleased he was going to actually meet with Daddy, whose legend was already growing. The day came. Earl dressed to the nines as only he could and showed up twenty minutes early at The Company. To his dismay, he was told that Daddy got called out of town and that he would meet with one of his lieutenants, Mr. Z. For thirty minutes, the conversation went well. At that point, Earl figured he would drop a name to help solidify his position.

"Mr. Z," he said, "I want you to know that I'm friends with Eddie."

Mr. Z went silent. Then a slight grin appeared on his face. "Try another name," he suggested as he began to laugh.

Earl couldn't help but laugh, too. This occasion may have been the first, but it would not be the last time he made the mistake of dropping Eddie's name.

The Company hired Earl, and he reported to work immediately. Each day, Eddie, Mr. Miller, and Earl went to lunch together, almost always to the Have-A-Bite Eatery, a small, local Greek restaurant. The conversation generally centered on the mortgage banking industry and the incredible cast of characters who made a living in it. For example, speaking of characters, some yoyo was running around Fairfax County with a rate sheet that said, "Shop Integrity, not rates." Really? What if a homebuyer called a realtor and asked if she could get a rate quote from this guy? The realtor says his rates aren't good, but he has a ton of integrity. Where would one suppose that was going to end up? Then there was the dynamic duo of two realtors who billed themselves as the "Sold Brothers." A take-off on the Blues Brothers, whom they dressed up as for their business card photos. If a couple is searching for a realtor to help them with the biggest purchase of their lives, are they more apt to hire a professional or a couple of clowns who can sing "Soul Man"? A pair to beat a full house. And, of course, one cannot forget the loan officer who called herself the "Loan Arranger." You guessed it. She had a rate sheet with a picture of the Masked One with his trusted sidekick Tonto next to a peppermint that she glued to the paper. People weren't actually begging this jabroni to finance their dream home. One wonders if she referred to her loan processor as Kemosabe.

Everybody seemed to know everybody else, especially if you had been in the business for a while. Add that it was such a transient business, and there was a good chance at some point you would end up working with people who had been competitors.

Autumn of 1988 rolled around, and things were going reasonably well. Daddy continued to hire more and more originators, filling the office to capacity. Daddy made plans to move to a brand-new facility sometime in 1989. Daddy's new hires were principally from the vast pool of loan originators operating in the Northern Virginia area. These people came from all walks of life. It became apparent that their methods of origination and salesmanship were highly diverse. In short, a fascinating crew was assembling, a fact not lost on the Bugeaters, with conversation increasingly focused on the daily activity at The Company.

There was plenty to talk about.

Every day was a new adventure. Earl's wife used to tell people how Earl loved going into the office because something crazy or funny would happen every day. Originators BS-ed borrowers, realtors, and themselves. Rarely would you find loan officers holding back on letting you know how much money they made last month. Most of the numbers were, of course, grossly inflated. If you added up the loan origination volume purportedly closed by Northern Virginia loan originators in any given year, it would eclipse that of the entire continental United States. The Bugeaters were clearly enjoying the joke in the spirit of frat house and locker room humor at its best!

With the holiday season fast approaching, Eddie came into work one day and walked into Earl's office.

"Hey Earl," he crowed. "What do you think of this expensive new suit?"

"Looks nice, Eddie," said Earl. "Proud as a peacock."

Eddie fired back, "Yeah, well, it's a Zsa-VONN-zsgee."

"Say what?"

"Zsay-VONN-zsgee!"

Earl almost split a gut laughing. "That's Givenchy, you fuckin' idiot," he retorted.

Earl couldn't wait to tell the rest of the crew about this one. Of course, henceforth, Eddie was known as Givenchy – pronounced: "Zsay-VONN-zsgee."

One day in early December, the Bugeaters convened for lunch. They had been discussing setting up a dinner before Christmas to establish the club membership and to hand out several fictitious awards honoring members' misdeeds and gaffes. The most prestigious award would naturally be Mortgage Banker of the Year, recognizing the loan officer who screwed up the most. Earl noted that the club needed a name. Eddie had one: The Bugeater Lunch and Supper Club. This name was in honor of his maternal grandfather, who had played football for the University of Nebraska in 1904 when the team was known as The Bugeaters. Earl and Mr. Miller agreed that it was a great name; therefore, it was adopted. Eddie was named Chairman, Earl, Secretary, and Mr. Miller, Treasurer. The Bugeater Lunch and Supper Club was official and operational.

They set the first meeting for the evening of December 20 at P.J. Skidoos, a local restaurant and pub. Fifteen members showed up for a few rounds of drinks and a nice dinner. The group was in a jovial, spirited mood. Business was good. Daddy's machine was chugging along, enhancing The Company and, therefore, the originators' reputations and pocketbooks.

Givenchy called the meeting to order. The primary order of business was to select the Mortgage Banker of the Year.

First vote: Eddie

Second Vote: Eddie

Third vote: Eddie

Fourteen votes for Eddie. Johnny Gumba was the last vote. A big hitter who had recently joined The Company, Daddy was grooming Gumba to be the next branch manager.

Johnny Gumba stood up and said, "I see you have a viable candidate for this envious award. However, I want to relate a story to you about one of your other colleagues. Please withhold your final vote until I am finished."

Gumba had visited The Company on a Tuesday afternoon in May before joining. After meeting with Daddy, he stopped in to visit with Mookie, a fellow loan officer who had been there a while. Mookie was on the phone talking to one of his borrowers. He motioned for Johnny to come into his office and sit down. He put the customer on the phone speaker box so Gumba could hear the conversation.

"I have some great news for you," Mookie said. "Your loan has been approved."

The customer was very pleased.

"There are three loan conditions we must meet so we can get you to settlement on Friday," Mook noted. "I need you to forward me your most recent paystub, your most recent complete checking account statement, and you need to get married this week."

They heard the air being sucked out of the phone, followed by the customer's choked voice. "Excuse me?"

"Yeah, VHDA loans require you to be married so we can count both incomes."

"But we're not getting married until fall," cried the poor borrower on the phone speaker box.

"No problem," said Mook. "Get your tails down to a justice of the peace ASAP and get hitched. Get me a marriage certificate, and we'll close your loan. Don't tell anybody you got married and have your ceremony in a couple of months. Nobody will be the wiser."

Gumba shared such a good story (Mookie was falling off his chair laughing when he hung up the phone) that it earned Mookie the first Mortgage Banker of the Year Award! Even though it was a massive upset over Eddie, the membership knew he would come back strong to win the award someday. Little did they know that Eddie would exceed their wildest expectations.

Earl, as club secretary, felt that the award winner should receive something to remember their accomplishments. He decided a commemorative plaque was in order and went to a local trophy shop to have one made up. It was very sharp. It showed a banker type in a three-piece suit, briefcase in hand, walking down a city street. Specifics on the plate included The Bugeater Lunch and Supper Club, the appropriate year, Mortgage Banker of the Year, and the winner's name. Mookie was quite proud.

The New Year came, and business continued to go well. The Company moved to its spanking-new office in March. Daddy's gig continued to attract originators from all over the area, providing fresh candidates for Bugeater membership. For the Club, 1989 proved equivalent to the best NFL or NBA draft years ever, seeing the debut of several future Mortgage Banker of the Year winners. Had a Bugeater Hall of Fame existed, these newcomers would have found their way there. The amount and degree of tomfoolery prompted the Bugeater leadership to adopt several new awards to be voted on and bestowed upon worthy recipients at the annual awards dinner.

The list is as follows:

Realtor of the Year: Similar to the Mortgage Banker award, presented to the realtor who goofed up consistently and exemplified an excess of the questionable traits many realtors possessed. These antics would include though not be limited to, the constant and incessant badgering of loan originators.

Client of the Year: The borrower (could be more than one) who brought the most misery down upon any given loan officer. Some borrowers would apply with two or three lenders at the same time and play one against the other. They would close with one near the settlement date and leave the others in the mud.

Rookie of the Year: The Bugeater standing out in the crop of rookies who showed the most promise in earning future awards (as noted, 1989 was off the charts). That crop was strong enough that one almost captured the coveted Mortgage Banker of the Year Award, an unheard-of feat.

Mr. Clean Award: Loan officer whose borrower(s) had the worst credit report. Loan officers knew they had a problem when realtors referred clients and characterized them as "good people."

Hourglass Award: Longest loan application taken by an originator. The leadership would actually time loan applications, so there was no fudging. The classic case was one of the Bugeaters going to the home of some applicants at 10 p.m. on a Wednesday night. The aunt and uncle were co-signing for the newlyweds. In addition to having to fill out four applications, the uncle decided to fire up a hash pipe and offer it to all the participants.

The Columbo Award: Best investigative work by a loan officer. For example, one of the Bugeaters camped out in an H&R Block office to analyze a borrower's tax returns. His diligence earned him the award and also the nickname "Columbo."

The Eddie Haskell Award: For *Leave It to Beaver* fans, this is a no-brainer. For newer generations, think of the loan officer who is the biggest BS artist in Northern Virginia. It is not a coincidence that Haskell and Eddie share the same first name. Eddie could sell fur coats in Miami and ice cubes at the North Pole.

The Phi Slamma Jamma Award: The loan officer who was able to jam the largest overage on a customer. This coup involved overcharging the customer and splitting the additional proceeds with The Company. This practice became so rampant that, at one point, the Federal Government limited the allowable amount of overage on certain types of loans and eventually curtailed it all together.

The Salvation Army Award: The loan officer forced to provide the largest subsidy on a loan. One could say the customer jammed the originator, making him or her take it in the shorts. Many originators put out false quotes on rate sheets to attract business, and at times, a realtor and borrower would force them to honor the low rate – resulting in a huge loss to the originator and The Company.

The Giorgio Armani Award: Self-explanatory. Best-dressed mortgage banker. A rookie showed up one day in a multi-colored plaid sports coat, which blew the Bugeaters away.

The Gerry's Ford Award: The loan officer who most closely resembled a used car salesman. Some originators would sell loan programs to borrowers knowing that the rate would eventually adjust to the point where they would have to come back for a refinance – one way to double the business.

The Pontius Pilate Award: The loan officer who washed their hands of the loan file after they turned it into processing. Took no further responsibility, ignored phone calls, and hoped the loan would close so he or she would get paid the commission. There was never a shortage of candidates for this award.

The Processor of the Year: Loan processor who screwed up the most, making their loan officers' lives miserable. Some processors would not work on cases until the day before settlement, then would force the loan officer to contact the borrowers and request a bunch of additional information – not exactly the way to enhance the originator's reputation.

The Joan of Arc Award: To the most martyred loan processor who had to work with and endure the biggest clowns (originators). Charli, a model of strength and perseverance, was granted a Lifetime Achievement Award for this category. As incredible as it may seem, she simultaneously processed for three Mortgage Banker of the Year Award winners. May she be granted eternal peace!

The Bugeaters, a pretty diverse group to begin with, took a diverse approach to the awards list and how they might qualify for it. Some relished the thought of winning an award – or awards! – and appreciated the humor surrounding them. Others didn't want to be named; they considered the awards derogatory and embarrassing. And then there were those so clueless they didn't know what to think.

Regardless, The Bugeaters adopted the awards list and put it in place. It would remain the foundation of The Bugeater Lunch and Supper Club for as long as it existed. The three charter members were pleased with what they had created ("and saw that it was good," to quote a line from the Bible!) and woke up every morning wondering: "What the hell is going to happen today? And who is going to become a legend as a result?"

Chapter 3

What's in a Name?

Earl grew up in Boston. Without exception, he calls every friend and person he knows by their nickname rather than by their given name. Some of them even have two or three nicknames. It's a custom they brought into the Bugeater Club; for whatever reason, everybody came up with a nickname for something somebody did or what they looked like, which is how nicknames go.

Daddy

- the patriarch of the mortgage banking industry in the metro DC area
- the patriarch of the Bugeater company
- a father figure to many of the company employees
- generous to a fault
- older than most of the other employees
- started the company
- he was Daddy!

Especially being a fast-buck business, people come and go at the drop of a hat. But Daddy had people who stayed with him for decades because of his generosity and being a father figure.

Eddie the Pec
- His first name is Edward, and the Pec is a take-off on "Jesse 'The Body' Ventura," the former governor from Minnesota, but that's where the resemblance stopped.
- They could have called him Eddie the Tricep or Eddie the Bicep. But Eddie the Pec sounded better.

Earl
- Thought to be "the sane guy in the insane asylum."
- All his Boston friends, UMass frat brothers, and the Bugeaters call him Earl (given name).
- His mother wanted to name him Patrick because he was born on St. Patrick's Day. However, his father's name is Earl, so he won out. Then his mother said, "Okay, I'll go with Earl, but we're going to call him Earl Richard, then we'll call him Rick."
- Being born in Boston on St. Patrick's Day is like royalty because forty percent of the city is Irish. One of Earl's mother's friends (his "aunt") was an Irish lady, and she was ecstatic when Earl was born on St. Patrick's Day.

Reverend
- He had signed up for the seminary when he was going to go to school before joining the Bugeaters, and then he bailed out of that to get into a more profitable career.
- In addition to his religious leanings, Reverend looks like a man of the cloth, like he'd be very comfortable in a parson's suit and hat.

Johnny Gumba
- You only had to look at him to understand why he was known as Johnny Gumba.
- He shaved twice a day because of his five o'clock shadow.
- His name was John, so they used to call him Johnny, and Earl came up with Gumba for the Italian thing.

Bow the Clown Prince
- He was as bow-legged as any cowboy ever seen in a Western movie.
- When Bow met Eddie the Pec, the first time he looked at him, Eddie said, "Did you sit on a horse for six months?" This guy's like a circle.

- "Clown Prince" because he represented everything wrong with mortgage banking. His motto was, "An ignorant consumer is my best customer."

Tim
- Every bit as Italian-looking as his older brother Johnny Gumba.
- Reverend somehow thought his name was Tim. He came up to Earl one day and said, "Hey, can we invite Tim to lunch?" Earl laughed and said, "Who the hell is Tim?" Reverend said, "Oh, you know, Johnny's little brother." Earl said, "You've got to be joking. You think that WOP's name is Tim? Okay, let's call him Tim." It made no sense at all, but it was consistent with a lot of things in the Bugeater world.

Wall Street Joe
- It's fair to say that there aren't a lot of country bumpkins from West Virginia named Wall Street Joe. Hayseed Joe, Mountain Joe, perhaps Country Joe. Once again, a name that was 180 degrees away from what it should have been.
- Wall Street Joe was a good guy but kind of a simpleton and a country boy.

Eskimo
- Could have been snowman or blow boy, maybe midnight coker. It certainly had nothing to do with Native American heritage; he was a toot king, pure and simple.

Colombo
- America's all-time favorite TV detective was the Bugeater's Colombo, so named as he camped out in an H&R Block office to investigate a client's tax returns. Apparently, he couldn't get the tax returns from the client. So, he went to the H&R Block office and just sat there until somebody would help him. Finally, he spent a whole day there. The

only way he could close the loan was if he got those tax returns. As the old saying goes, "No closing, no commission, no ticky, no laundry." Hence Colombo.

Charli
- Back in the day, when she was processing for the Bugeaters, they probably should have called her Joan, short for Joan of Arc. She is the most martyred loan processor in the history of The Company. Charli was a trouper.
- At one time, she simultaneously worked for three Mortgage Bankers of the Year.
- It's all right there.

Mr. Miller
- Mr. Miller was Mr. Miller.
- They called him Mister as a sign of respect since he was the Bugeater treasurer, even though the Bugeaters had no funds to manage.

Ab La Sword
- La Sword was actually close to the pronunciation of his real name.
- Ab was short for Abner, the most obnoxious name the Bugeaters could come up with for their favorite whipping boy.
- He was a whipping boy. Everybody needs one, right?

Big Marvin
- Big Marvin was big. He clocked in at almost three bills, 300 pounds.
- Marvin was also close to his real last name.

Dee
- Johnny Gumba's paramour and eventual wife. Her first name began with a D. And it is also appropriate in that divorce also begins with a D, which was the net result of this nefarious relationship.

Nate
- Nate is a female and an abbreviation of her real last name.
- Earl called her Nathan, taking the name and extending it as a more formal approach.

Carol
- Carol was Carol's name.
- It's very appropriate that Carol is a woman's or a man's name, as the Bugeater's Carol was a man in a woman's body. She was actually rougher than the rest of them.

B.B.
- B.B. were his real initials. Not for Bird Brain, although it might have been appropriate, as at one time, he fell off a third-floor balcony in Cancun and landed on his head. True story. Earl thinks the only thing that kept him going was he swilled down a quart of tequila before he fell off.

Barry Seeless
- The company's appraiser on occasion. He would bring in an appraisal $200 low, which prompted the Bugeaters to wonder what he was looking at.
- In other words, the "see less" kind of thing.

Mookie
- There was one famous Major League Baseball player named Mookie.
- This guy was a fan and also, his last name was the ball player's name.

The Zealist
- Close to his real last name.
- He was a zealot in many ways, a political zealot, anything and everything.

Mr. Z
- Mister as a sign of respect, and Z was his last name's initial

Sean
- Sean because he claimed on a company trip to the Bahamas that he played golf with and procured the autograph of Sean Connery. Something closer to the truth would be that Sean Connery was on the island at the same time.

Chapter 4

Wilbon

In the mortgage banking business, you never know who you might end up putting in a house.

Loan originators perform many duties and have certain responsibilities. But at the end of the day, they are salesmen. And like all salesmen, they adopt a method and a plan as to how they will go about stimulating sales.

Many of the Bugeaters entered the mortgage banking industry in the mid-to-late '80s when the traditional method of soliciting business was through the realtor community. Droves of loan officers would descend on real estate offices daily to hand out their rate sheets. They would try to come up with something new to talk about since they would constantly encounter the same realtors. It was not very comforting upon entering a real estate office to be greeted by the desk duty agent who informed you that you were the fifteenth loan originator to visit before lunchtime.

Eddie the Pec had developed a good set of skills while selling for Xerox. He realized early on as a mortgage banker that the industry's traditional sales methods were not for him. There were two reasons for this position. First, he realized it would benefit him to stand out from the rest of the pack of loan originators buzzing around Northern Virginia. Second, he came to deplore soliciting and working with most realtors. Eddie considered their loyalty to be on par with pigeons chirping through a city park looking for the next passerby to throw them a scrap of food. As in, they would leave the guy with popcorn for a ritz cracker from someone else.

However, one of his most loyal and best-known customers came to him in a way he could never have foreseen.

One of the original mortgage loan officers hired by The Company, Eddie, hailed from O'Neill, Nebraska. O'Neill is also the birthplace of Frank Leahy, the legendary Notre Dame football coach from the 1940s through 1953.

Eddie's father, a Nebraska native, was a diehard Subway Alumni Irish fan in the middle of Cornhusker country. Meanwhile, the younger Eddie was an avid Nebraska fan, which led to considerable friction between father and son. Often on the same weekend, The Doctor, a dentist, and the mayor of O'Neill would travel by train to Chicago and on to South Bend with his fellow Notre Dame buddies to see the Irish. Eddie, just in grade school in the mid-'60s, would sneak onto a bus loaded with local Husker fans for the 200-mile trek for the weekly big home game in Memorial Stadium.

On the Monday following the games, there was always an ongoing argument between father and son as to who supported the better team. Granted, Notre Dame had more tradition and history, but Nebraska was on the rise as a true national power thanks to their coach, Bob Devaney. In 1970 and 1971, Nebraska won back-to-back national championships. Notre Dame won national championships under the legendary Ara Parseghian in 1966 and 1973. So, who had the better program?

Nebraska was matched against Notre Dame in the Orange Bowl on New Year's Day following the 1972 season – a match made in heaven and in The Doctor's household. The younger Eddie was set with tickets for the game but could not convince his father to go along. His father must have had an inkling of what would happen in Miami.

Heisman Trophy winner Johnny Rodgers led the Huskers, scored four touchdowns, and passed for another to completely annihilate the under-matched Irish, 40-6!!! It was the end of The Doctor's dominance in the Irish-Husker discussions. In fact, The Doctor slowly drifted from being a diehard Irish fan to a very avid Husker fan.

The young Eddie moved away from Nebraska after college and settled in the Nation's Capital to seek his fame and fortune. After a saloon job or two, he went to work for one of the premier marketing firms in the country, selling for Xerox. After eight years, Eddie moved on to mortgage banking, hoping to utilize his sales skills in a relatively new and upcoming industry. He met "Daddy," and his new career took off with one of the best industry leaders in the country.

While living far from Middle America, Eddie still managed to travel west to attend the Nebraska-Oklahoma game and the Nebraska-Colorado game wherever they played. Despite a string of almost twenty years of mediocrity, his love and passion for the Huskers never diminished – his passion only grew stronger.

One day in December 1993, as Eddie was planning his annual trip to watch the Huskers in a New Year's Day Bowl game, Earl shared an article published in the Washington Post. The Huskers were matched up against the No. 1 team in the country, Florida State, led by Heisman Trophy winner Charlie Ward. The game was for the BCS (Bowl Championship Series) championship with the winner to be declared No. 1.

Nebraska had finally made it back to the pinnacle after twenty years.

A columnist from the Post, Michael Wilbon, took dead aim at the Huskers. He torched the team, the fans, and the program in general. Now, in fairness, the Huskers had lost their previous seven bowl games to speedy Southern teams, but the column went out of its way to insult Nebraska football.

Eddie felt his world turned upside down. How could such a respected and famous columnist do this to such a storied program?

Eddie reacted by calling Wilbon's voicemail at the Post. Forgetting his past respect and admiration for the Post columnist, and with Earl's prodding, Eddie ripped into Wilbon, cursing, threatening bodily injury, and insulting Wilbon's credibility. Arriving home that evening, Eddie found several return messages on his answering machine from Wilbon. They were equally insulting and pretty much repeated what he had written in the column. Eddie took the recordings from Wilbon and sent them to a friend, who happened to be the program director at the Cornhuskers' flagship radio station. Thousands of Husker fans heard Wilbon's rants for nearly two weeks prior to the Orange Bowl. Wilbon could not have been more pleased with his sudden notoriety in Nebraska.

Entering the game, the Huskers were a 17-point underdog to Florida State, with plenty of fools willing to give the 17 points and take Florida State. Eddie had no problem taking those bets. In the end, Nebraska lost by two points on a last-second missed field goal. It was an incredibly tight game.

Eddie was terribly upset by the loss, but the bump to his bank account brought about by the point spread tempered the defeat.

Fast-forward nearly a year to Halloween weekend. Eddie was making his annual trip to the Colorado-Nebraska game in Lincoln that weekend. The game was huge. Colorado, led by Kordell Stewart and Michael Westbrook, was ranked No. 1, the Huskers No. 3. It was early Friday morning, and Eddie was sitting in the back of a plane at Reagan National Airport with very few people on the flight. Just before takeoff, Wilbon boarded the plane and took his seat in first class.

Eddie immediately spotted Wilbon and scribbled some unkind words on a napkin. He gave it to a flight attendant to pass on to Wilbon.

The first leg of the flight went to Chicago with a two-hour layover. About halfway to Chicago, Eddie could no longer contain himself. He made his way up to first class and found Wilbon stretched out, sound asleep. Finally, he awakened Wilbon and introduced himself. Wilbon knew who Eddie was immediately. Eddie's Midwestern upbringing took over, and he was a complete gentleman. Eddie had enjoyed and respected Wilbon's writing and opinions for many years and was in awe at finally meeting him face to face. They ultimately had a cordial fifteen-minute conversation and shook hands before Eddie had to return to his seat as the plane approached Chicago.

Eddie was the last person off the plane and found Wilbon waiting for him. Since there was a lengthy layover, Wilbon invited Eddie to breakfast. It was the beginning of a long friendship. The conversation, of course, was all about sports and Nebraska football. On their way to the departure gate, Wilbon asked for Eddie's ticket to upgrade him to first class so they could sit together. Wilbon said he planned to interview a Nebraska fan for Saturday's article in the Post. So, during the entire second leg of the flight, which ended in Omaha, Wilbon quizzed Eddie on the history of fan support for the Huskers, the reasons why fans were so rabid, and to understand better how people could be so obsessed. Upon arrival, Eddie introduced his newfound friend to all of his buddies who showed up at the airport, including a former Husker player, the biggest bookie in the Midwest, and a few relatives. They all knew who Wilbon was and what he had written and said about the Huskers, so they were understandably a little standoffish. They all wondered how Eddie could even talk to the guy who had completely trashed everything about the state of Nebraska. But like most Midwesterners, they were genuinely cordial to Wilbon. Eddie urged patience and promised a complete change in Wilbon's attitude toward Nebraskans.

The next morning, the most heartfelt and wonderful article appeared in the Post and other syndicated newspapers across the country, including the Omaha World-Herald. As promised, Eddie transformed Wilbon's attitude about Nebraska, and he got his proverbial "fifteen minutes of fame" in Nebraska and at home in Northern Virginia.

The game was the frosting on the cake for the weekend. Nebraska clobbered Colorado 24-13. The game was not as close as the score would indicate. Nebraska went on to capture the Big 8 title and ended up playing the Miami Hurricanes in the Orange Bowl. Tom Osborne won his first of three national championships at Nebraska. Wilbon again gave the Huskers, their fans, and the entire state their just due with another column the day after the game.

Starting from a nasty, scathing column, Wilbon experienced a complete attitude change. More importantly, a genuine friendship began, which lasts through today and several new homes. Eddie picked up a new friend and a valued mortgage customer as well!

The Washington Post

HUSKERS: SAME OLD SHUCK, JIVE

By MICHAEL WILBON
November 16, 1993

Fortunately, people are a lot less accepting of junk than they used to be. Even sports junk. There's so much on TV now, whether over-the-air or cable, that it's easy to just say no and flick over to something else. This, sooner than later, is going to make pay-per-view mandatory. You have to give the people what they want, or they'll flick you off. This brings us to college football. We're no longer in an era when you can throw Keith Jackson behind the microphone at some three-yards-and-a- cloud-of-dust sleepathon and make people watch simply because we're high and mighty college football so take it or leave it. People will leave it, unless it's compelling. College football came to this realization a couple of years ago when they formed the Bowl Coalition, a fairly clever gimmick designed to avoid a college football playoff.

It can work. It did last year when we got Miami vs. Alabama on New Year's night. And it can work again this year, as long as we get the best matchup possible. That, at the moment, would appear to be Notre Dame vs. Florida State. Or Florida State vs. the Miami/West Virginia winner. My scenarios do not, under any circumstances, include Nebraska. Thankfully, the media types who vote in the Associated Press poll rescued us (for now) by counteracting the coaches in the CNN-USA Today Football Coaches poll. The coaches say Nebraska, 10-0, is No. 2 in the nation; the media says Nebraska is No. 3. Taken vote by vote, Nebraska slips to No. 3 in the all-important bowl coalition poll.

A few years back, I was an AP voter. It's a good thing I no longer have a vote. I'd make sure, personally, Nebraska had no chance of fouling up the national championship picture by voting the Huskers, say, No. 68. Nebraska, you see, is the second biggest fraud in college football every single solitary season. Michigan is Fraud #1. Together, they stack up all-Americans five deep at every position, then choke on New Year's Day. You can make the case (and I often do) that Michigan and Nebraska football are the most overrated teams in all of sports. Any sport. Nobody chokes more. Fortunately, we don't have to waste any more breath on Michigan, which was done weeks ago.

Oklahoma could save us from a holiday nightmare by laying waste to Nebraska. Here is Nebraska's recent bowl history: six straight losses by an average of 17.7 points. If it's not for LSU acting like a doormat in two Sugar Bowls (1985 and 1987), Nebraska is 0-for-a-decade. It started in '84 when the Cornhuskers lost the Orange Bowl to Miami, 31-30, in one of the most memorable games of all time. Okay, there's nothing to be ashamed about there, or in the Losers Bowl loss to Michigan (1986 Fiesta), 27-23.

Since, there's been a three-point loss to Florida State in the Fiesta, a 20-3 loss to Miami in the Orange, a 41-17 loss to Florida State in the Fiesta, a 45-32 loss to Georgia Tech in the Citrus, a 22-0 loss to Miami in the

Orange and a 27-14 loss to Florida State (again) in the Orange. That's 189 to 83 if you're scoring in aggregate. Nebraska gets in a New Year's Day Bowl, Nebraska stinks the joint out. There's no other conclusion.

Now it's no real shock that the coaches have voted Nebraska No. 2. Nebraska is undefeated and coached by Tom Osborne, a respected member of the coaching profession. To vote Nebraska third would be perceived as some indictment of Osborne and his coaching philosophy. The members of the media (who vote in the AP poll) hold no such allegiance to Osborne. I, for one, am in favor of a two-year ban from all press boxes any reporter who votes Nebraska No. 2.

Do you really want to see Florida State trash Nebraska for the umpteenth time? Or would you like a legitimate sports event on New Year's night, or maybe even Jan. 2 after the NFL games since NBC would probably want a special showcase for a title game? My worry is that Florida, almost impossible to beat at home, is going to beat Florida State in two weeks, the game being played in Gainesville. That might allow Miami's Hurricanes to slip up to No. 2, except that Miami is going to lose Saturday at West Virginia.

It amuses me how many people are picking Miami to win in a rout. In Morgantown. Hey, these aren't Jimmy Johnson's Hurricanes, or the even the Jimmy Johnson recruits Dennis Erickson used to win his first couple of seasons. Erickson isn't Howard Schnellenberger and he isn't J.J. Miami is still a great team, but nobody is literally afraid of the Hurricanes anymore, like basketball teams used to be afraid to play Georgetown for fear of being embarrassed. The fact that the AP poll has West Virginia No. 9 (behind Florida and Tennessee) speaks to media bias against West Virginia. The knock is West Virginia's schedule, which is ridiculous considering the Big East is getting better and the Mountaineers have beaten some good teams, including Louisville and Syracuse.

The team we haven't mentioned, and really shouldn't waste time with, is Ohio State -- only because the Buckeyes are locked into the Rose Bowl playing some inconsequential Pac-10 team in an inconsequential game for what seems like the 20th year in a row. Auburn-Florida State would be interesting, pitting the Daddy Bowden against Baby Bowden, but Auburn is on probation. (Is there a year A.D. when either Auburn or Clemson wasn't on probation?)

When the dust clears a week from Saturday, I expect Notre Dame to be undefeated and Florida State to have narrowly beaten Florida in a game every bit as good as Notre Dame-FSU. This postgame trashing of Florida State, in the wake of Saturday's loss in South Bend, is petty and stupid. There's never been a team in the history of football that should beat an undefeated Notre Dame team playing at home. Never. FSU didn't choke or lose the big one. The Seminoles lost by one play to a team that is equally talented. To call Notre Dame's victory an upset would be unspeakably naive.

With the NFL trying to find somebody worthy of challenging the Cowboys and with the NBA reloading in the wake of losing Magic, Bird and Jordan, sports junkies are in need of a fix, the big event. That's why so many people watched Notre Dame-FSU on Saturday. This notion that a team should only get one chance, that

rematches are only for the pros, sounds like some purist nonsense. If that's part of college football "tradition" we'd better start along a new sensible path. If the pollsters and the bowl people can't give us Notre Dame and Florida State again, we can just find something else to watch or do on a Saturday night. Can't we?

💬 Comments

The BUGEATER LUNCH and SUPPER CLUB

The Washington Post

SAY HELLO TO OBSESSION

By MICHAEL WILBON
October 29, 1994

LINCOLN, NEB. -- People talk all the time about big games and crazy scenes and local folk obsessed with the home team, but they haven't seen anything until they've been here, to Nebraska, on the weekend of a big game. Or for that matter, the weekend of a small game. You grow up and live your life in the big city, in New York or Los Angeles or Chicago or D.C., you have no idea what total sports obsession is about. Nebraska knows obsession. Saturday, Memorial Stadium will be sold out for the 200th consecutive time, dating from 1962. Funerals and weddings will be put on hold until the game -- maybe even the entire weekend -- is over. All 3,000 hotel rooms here have been sold, and probably twice that many 50 miles east in Omaha.

It's like this every time the Cornhuskers put on uniforms; they even sell out the spring games -- that's 72,700 plus standing room. It's even more berserk than usual because Saturday's opponent is Colorado, Public Enemy No. 1, a neighbor absolutely unwelcome. This is big. You think Redskins-Cowboys is big? It isn't. It's Muggsy Bogues. Nebraska-Colorado is Gheorghe. Any bigger and it would eclipse the sun. Local businessmen are upset that the game is starting two hours earlier than usual (11 a.m. Central time for national TV), which might make a dent in the $1 million in receipts they realize on a normal game day.

At least one pregame show will begin at 8 a.m., and the procession from Omaha to Lincoln will clog the interstate beginning, the locals warn, at 6:30 a.m. John Harris, the special assistant to the vice chancellor for student affairs, was conducting a recent retreat for students and asked a question that made each and every one of them recoil in horror. "I asked them, 'Suppose there was no Nebraska football? Suppose for some reason the school had to do away with it?' Their first response was shock, like, 'How could he dare ask that question, even think it?' You know what? It would destroy the economy of the school, of the state. Everything we do here at the university is scheduled around football, from the chancellor on down. At the end of every summer, you know what people are doing? Longing. Salivating. This is the gospel, this is the truth right here. For these people to be without Nebraska football is to be without sustenance."

Nebraska football fans are about the most loyal, knowledgeable, supportive, overly sensitive, pain-in-the-butt fans you can imagine, which I found out the hard way a year ago. In a column, I dared call the Cornhuskers, who turn into doormats on New Year's Day, one of the two biggest frauds in all of college football, Michigan being the other. I got a grand total of three letters from Michigan fans. As for Nebraska fans, I stopped counting the faxes, letters, hand-delivered packages, threatening phone calls and unannounced visits to my office when the number passed 500. I was officially reprimanded by the D.C.-area Nebraska alums. Two TV stations wanted to fly me to the next Huskers game, put me up for the weekend and follow me around campus. Two radio stations woke me during morning drive time with the Nebraska fight song playing in my ear through the telephone.

Through the expletives and threats, I got to know and really like one caller, Michael Gleeson, a mortgage loan officer in Fairfax, a sportsaholic whose knowledge, particularly about football, is encyclopedic, and who was completely charming as long as those two paragraphs from a year ago didn't come up. Gleeson and I were on the same flight from D.C. to Lincoln Friday morning. I told him I was trying to understand what it is about Nebraska fans that makes them so different from even Alabama, Auburn, Clemson or Tennessee fans.

Gleeson had stories, dozens of stories. His grandfather played for Nebraska in 1904 when they were called the "Bugeaters." Gleeson has been to 32 consecutive Nebraska-Colorado games, but tells the story about his cousin, Jean Devoy, a school teacher who has paid her own way to every road game since 1965 -- bowl games, games in Hawaii, doesn't matter. Her whole house is decorated in red-and-white, Huskers colors. Coaches over the years have all known her by first name because she attends the breakfast meetings the coaches have with the public a couple of times a week. Breakfast meetings?

"The answer," Gleeson said, "is pretty simple. We don't have anything else. I've been a Redskins fan for 20 years. People talk about Washington being obsessed with the Redskins, but comparing it to Nebraska and the Cornhuskers, it's not even close. Not close. I tell people in D.C. this and they think I'm crazy. I live and breathe Nebraska football. We all do."

Gleeson tells me a P.S. to his first phone call. He played my return message on his voice mail for the Nebraska football flagship station, and they put it on the air. Gleeson is one of those people who is plugged in, wise, smart. Just got married, bought his parents a house, got a couple of new dogs. But don't criticize the Huskers. "I get more intense every year," he said. "And every year I say I'm going to stop it, calm down, not be such a fanatic. But like everybody else here, I got hooked when {Bob} Devaney's teams won those national championships. And every year, I keep wanting and searching. Tom Osborne has broken my heart every time. I love him, but I'm a betting man too. And I'm from Nebraska. We take it so seriously because we don't have anything else. We get so defensive. I see it in myself. You think I'm fanatical? I'm mild. And most of 'em just get to listen to the games on radio, at best. Most people never go. There's no tickets available, unless you go buy one {scalped} for several hundred dollars. They've never been. The ones who do go, the farmers, they sit there in the bitter cold and they just love it."

Gleeson, like so many other Nebraskans, can recall every critical word from those two paragraphs a year ago. They get angry, but then they offer to send you a Big Red sweatshirt. Or they have their nephew who once played as a walk-on call you and tell you why Nebraska football is so great. Or they invite you to the Big Red breakfast at the Ramada, but you have to get there by 7 a.m. or you'll never get served in time for the game. Some of them drive 650 miles, one way, every week from the other corner of the state and they're totally euphoric every minute of the drive. They fill the restaurants and bars on Friday night, anxious and consumed. You look in their eyes and hear their conversations, all of it as real as life itself, and you just know you've

never heard or seen anything like them.

The BUGEATER LUNCH and SUPPER CLUB

NOTHING BUT GUTTER BALLS ON A DAY OF BOWLING - The... https://www.washingtonpost.com/archive/sports/1995/01/04/nothing-bu...

The Washington Post

NOTHING BUT GUTTER BALLS ON A DAY OF BOWLING

By MICHAEL WILBON
January 4, 1995

Tell the truth now. Did you stay up until all hours watching the final minutes of that last bowl game, as if it were election night? Did you sit there with the clicker in hand frantically surfing back and forth from the Cotton to the Citrus to the Hall of Fame to the CarQuest to the Fiesta to the Rose, trying to figure out who was still alive, who still was playing for the chance to be No. 1? Did you sit there with remnants of chips and dip all over your sweatshirt, phone on your shoulder, arguing with some fat slob neighbor about whether he should be waiting until halftime to join his wife in the delivery room?

Of course you didn't.

That's because The Great Bowl Day was a great waste of time.

We already knew Nebraska had won the national championship.

Don't tell me you've crowned a new champion one day and expect me to watch more games the next day. Watching bowl games on Monday was like trying to get into "extra time" in soccer. Personally, I don't think college football has an encore to Tommie Frazier. It's like going to a Streisand concert, then being asked to sit for a few tunes from Cyndi Lauper.

I tried to watch Monday, I tried to get into the spirit by ordering 11 pizzas from Dominos all for me. But I couldn't do it. Wound up switching over to HBO to watch "Love Potion No. 9." For the most part, I can't even tell who won, who lost or which teams played each other.

That is, for the most part. There are only two things memorable about Bowl weekend.

Nebraska won.

Notre Dame got clocked.

Both things are as they should be.

Now, you long-suffering Nebraska supporters, who are simultaneously the sweetest and most rabid people I've ever received hate mail from, are probably saying, "Don't tell me this guy, after trashing Nebraska for seven years, is going to say nice stuff about Dr. Tom and our Huskers!"

Of course I am! This is the way it works: If you lose, everybody says you're a choking dog. If you win, there's a

35

NOTHING BUT GUTTER BALLS ON A DAY OF BOWLING - The... https://www.washingtonpost.com/archive/sports/1995/01/04/nothing-bu...

parade and so much praise you'd think Tom Osborne discovered the cure for cancer.

Nebraska is No. 1 and there's simply no debate to be had. The Cornhuskers had a tougher schedule than Penn State, a lineup they not only mastered, but somehow negotiated with a backup quarterback for most of the season. They also played a tougher, higher-ranked bowl opponent, on the opponent's home field. They went to Miami and took a game, gangstered it really, in the fourth quarter when champions come to play. And in the end, they left the Orange Bowl looking like the better-coached and absolutely smarter team. While the Hurricanes were dancing around making fools of themselves for the TV cameras, losing energy all the while, the Huskers were conserving for the fourth quarter, plotting every move.

Osborne handled perfectly what could have been a quarterback nightmare. Just when the script was calling for Frazier to be reinserted, there was Dr. Tom tapping Frazier on the shoulder. Didn't you just get goosebumps? My first thoughts were of Huskers fan and my man Mike Gleeson, who missed his first Nebraska bowl game so he could stay home and be with his pregnant wife. You have to have been to Nebraska to appreciate what Sunday night meant to the entire state and its psyche. It's a state full of people who write nasty letters when you say one bad word about the Huskers, then invite you into their homes and offer to take you on a tour of the campus if you'll only come out and spend the weekend and enjoy the big game with them in Lincoln.

The only people who have suffered as much as Nebraskans are Bills fans. As much as I love the Hurricanes and their rebel mentality, I couldn't help but root for Osborne and the Huskers Sunday night because he is as decent a man as there is in college football, and he seems to run his program with as much care and integrity as does Joe Paterno or John Thompson or Dean Smith or Coach K. That and, well, I'm tired of having to console friends from Buffalo and Nebraska. And if you see any of those Big Red Championship T-shirts around, I'm an XXL.

Paterno's had his day, a couple of them, and will probably have more. Nobody in the Big Ten is an immediate long-term threat to Penn State, certainly not Michigan, which now stands by itself as the single most overrated football program in America. And I don't know about you, but I'm getting a little tired of the Florida schools. Can't anybody else in the country play this game besides the same tired 15 schools, all of whom were on my TV (overlapping no doubt) on Monday?

Personally, I'm glad The Great Bowl Day was a bust. This is exactly what the bowls deserve, considering its the most trumped-up, overhyped day this side of any heavyweight boxing match.

Why don't the powers that be in college football give us what we want, which is a national championship playoff system? I get a kick out of these two new arguments that have popped up to support the bowl system. The first is, "Well, the players themselves don't want a championship." Yeah, right. And the second is, "It's so much fun to debate all season who's No. 1. Why should one school have all the glory." Say what?

The BUGEATER LUNCH and SUPPER CLUB

NOTHING BUT GUTTER BALLS ON A DAY OF BOWLING - The...   https://www.washingtonpost.com/archive/sports/1995/01/04/nothing-bu...

Two words for you knuckleheads: March Madness.

The bottom line is, eight teams could play in seven games (bowl games if you will) for the national title over three weekends. They could play the championship game in Phoenix every year during the off-week between the NFL conference championship games and the Super Bowl. We'd all sit there riveted for every game and I'd bet you nobody would pick up the clicker and switch to "Love Potion No. 9."

💬 **Comments**

Chapter 5

Johnny Gumba

Johnny Gumba thought he was the most interesting man in mortgage banking.

Gumba, Eddie the Pec, and Reverend were driving down Route 66 one afternoon in Gumba's brand-new Mercedes-Benz. He had been having trouble with one of the wheels, leading to an uneven ride. Eddie wanted to gig him, so he commented on the situation.

Gumba exploded. "I've already had this goddamn rig back at that dealership four times. They've yet to straighten it out. Watch this." He dialed the dealership and reached the same service writer who had been allegedly trying to solve the problem. He put the phone on speaker. "This is Johnny Gumba," he snarled.

"How are you, Mr. Gumba?" the employee asked.

"Not real good. This piece of trash you sold me is still acting up. I'm done dealing with the likes of you. Put your fuckin' boss on the phone right now."

"Yes, sir," he responded meekly.

Two minutes later, the service manager came on the line. He identified himself and asked if he could be of any assistance.

Gumba was incensed. "Do you know who I am?" he screamed.

The manager hesitated, then wearily said, "No, but I'm sure you are about to tell me."

Gumba hailed from a small town in West Virginia. His father passed away when Gumba was a teenager, forcing him to grow up in a hurry. As the eldest son, he assumed patriarchal duties and had to find a way to support his mother, brother, and sister. And find a way he did by sharpening his sales skills by peddling some products of an infamous Italian organization (often running afoul of the law) that heavily influenced his area. Eventually, Johnny also ran afoul and went away for a vacation at the taxpayers' expense. No big deal – you did what you had to do.

Gumba went to college in his home state and got into mortgage banking shortly after finishing up. His cousin managed an outfit in Northern Virginia, and he convinced Johnny to sign up. His cousin did a ton of business, and ultimately, Gumba did as well. Like many successful business people, they carved out a niche for themselves, which made them unique.

They became well known for their ability to close mortgage loans on a moment's notice in an environment where the typical settlement took 60 days. Credit reports took two weeks to obtain – appraisals over a month. Employment and asset verifications were done by mail – fax machines did not exist. How did they do it? They just did it. Realtors would refer loans that needed a quick turnaround or loans that other lenders had trouble completing. Gumba and his cousin would close these loans without appraisals and the necessary verifications. They would then be hopeful they could obtain the required documentation post-closing. It was simply a numbers game. A small percentage of the loans were not saleable to the group of investors they usually sold loans to but paled in comparison to the overall volume they were doing. They would sell the "bad" loans for cents on the dollar to investors who bought that type of product. They could afford to take an occasional loss as the quid pro quo for their tremendous profits on their "good" loans. They were mortgage banking superheroes to the realtor community who knew they were guaranteed to get their commission if they referred a loan to them.

Daddy heard about the numbers Gumba and his cousin were putting up. He thought it would be a long shot to recruit the cousin because he was president of their company, but he figured he might have a chance with Gumba. It also didn't hurt that Daddy's CFO, Eskimo, was married to Johnny's cousin. Daddy called Eskimo into his office.

"What do you know about this character, Johnny Gumba?"

"Does big numbers," Eskimo said. "Big ego to go along with the big numbers."

Daddy had dealt with his share of big egos. This guy would be just another brick in the wall. "How's he doing that kind of volume?"

Eskimo smiled. "He and his cousin play the market and undercut everybody in town. His rate sheet is always a point less than the competition. They also will close anything on a moment's notice and try to clean it up on the back end."

Daddy knew how to play the market and could handle the discounted rates. He would not gamble on closing loans without the proper documentation but he could work around that. He told Eskimo to get Gumba in for an interview.

"Done," said Eskimo.

"Good deal," barked Daddy.

A week later, Gumba showed up at The Company for his interview dressed like a mafia don. Daddy ushered Gumba into his office, and the gentlemen sized each other up. It was essentially oil and water. Gumba didn't like hunting or fishing and would not spend his afternoons swilling down Kurz Laht. Daddy didn't care for Gumba's cocky manner or his extravagant lifestyle. But at the end of the day, Daddy was a bottom-line guy. He ponied up a sizeable signing bonus and the promise that Johnny would become the branch manager. It didn't matter that there was a branch manager in place. Such circumstances should never stand in the way of making money. They shook hands, which was notable because it was the first and last time they did.

Gumba reported for work and continued to originate loans at a record pace. Daddy let him operate with rates discounted by a point, which enhanced his production. But Johnny was profitable nonetheless. His ability to play the market and his willingness to jam overages on many customers contributed significantly to The Company's bottom line. His methods did not go unnoticed by the other loan originators. They knew the kind of money he was making, and the word got out that he was in line to take over as branch manager. The Bugeaters realized it was only a matter of time before they would fall under Gumba's wing. The intelligent members (of which there were a few) began establishing close relationships with Johnny in anticipation of things to come. If one had a crystal ball, they would have advised the Bugeaters to "hold on to your hats."

Saint Patrick's Day 1989 was notable for three reasons. First, it was Earl's 36th birthday. Being born in Boston on Saint Patty's was considered royalty. Second, The Company relocated to its new office location, and third, Johnny Gumba was officially named Branch Manager. Meanwhile, the incumbent manager was less than pleased when shuffled to a new position by Daddy. Gumba was ecstatic and primed to stamp his blueprint on The Company. He vowed to run the incumbent out of the organization, which happened sooner than even Johnny thought possible.

Gumba went about establishing his fiefdom as if he was a Sicilian Don. He did everything with a Machiavellian approach. He was very paranoid about intercompany relationships, especially those that involved Daddy. For example, when Reverend first came to The Company, Daddy learned he played golf in college, so he summoned Reverend to his office and informed him they would play golf. For money, of course. Reverend had no choice but to accept. When

Gumba found out about it, he became suspicious and irritated. He called Reverend in with the intent of firing him.

"I heard you have a meeting set up with Daddy," growled Gumba.

"A meeting? He wants to take my money on the golf course. What am I supposed to do?" asked Reverend.

Gumba stared at him, then looked out the window. He stared at Reverend again and said, "Okay. You can play with him and let him take what money you might have. But you will not talk to him. Am I clear?"

"Crystal clear," said Reverend. Now all he had to do was figure out how to spend five hours on a golf course with the man who owns The Company that employs him and not speak to him. It was all Reverend could do but wonder what the hell he had gotten himself into.

Reverend told Eddie about the absurd conversation he had just had with Johnny Gumba. Eddie vowed to exact revenge on Gumba. After hours that day, when he got home, he made sure his dog Jake was well-fed and then brought him to the office. Right on cue, as they entered Gumba's office, Jake relieved himself on Gumba's carpet. Johnny came in the next morning and managed to step into the mess. He was incensed and couldn't figure out if the mess was from a dog or a human. Was it from the incumbent manager he had just run off? If so, he would have him taken care of.

Johnny Gumba was making money hand over fist. As manager of one of the country's biggest volume mortgage banking firms, he certainly had power. What came next? The women, of course. Johnny did his best to perpetuate the myth that Italian men had insatiable sex drives. He hired a beautiful secretary who, in short order, was tending to his needs in the evening hours. He hired an assistant whose primary responsibility was to bring a cup of coffee to his office first thing in the morning and proceed to service him while he planned his busy day. He felt it was necessary to clear his mind. Unfortunately, it couldn't clear his nose from all the blow he had typically ingested the night before. Apparently, Johnny couldn't fit his pretty wife into his sexual schedule, which was confirmed when a landscape architect who Earl's wife knew and referred to the Gumbas, showed up at their home for a consultation. Johnny's wife was all over him and tried to drag him into the bedroom. Whether his reluctance to participate stemmed from his knowledge that she was a married woman or that he was gay remains to be seen. The bottom line was that he hightailed it out of there before he could discuss any shrubs or trees.

The Company hired a gorgeous new employee who eventually would change Gumba's life forever. She was a friend of Nate, a female employee who had started with The Company as a processor and had moved up to loan officer. The new hire had no knowledge of mortgage banking or anything else, for that matter. But, so what? Daddy had a habit of hiring people when he was out drinking if he liked their looks. They would show up for work without knowing what he had hired them to do. One of the department managers would park them at a desk where they could collect a paycheck as long as they stayed out of trouble. The new lady appeared to fit the bill. However, Nate, for one, should have known better.

That is because a short time before that, Gumba had lured Nate to his spacious home and informed her, "This can all be yours if you'll simply put out."

Nate rebuffed his advances and reported the incident to Daddy who was already growing tired of Johnny's antics. But Daddy was also aware of the bulging bottom line. So, he did what he always did when confronted with a sexual harassment issue. He wrote a check and made the problem go away.

Shortly thereafter, Gumba was sipping his morning coffee and making the rounds of The Company. He was in a good mood as he had just received his daily servicing. He passed by the processing bullpen, and there she sat. The new hire. He felt like he was just struck with a massive thunderbolt as "she was looking like a queen in a sailor's dream." Gumba rushed down to the processing manager's office and demanded, "Who the hell is that bombshell sitting in the bullpen?"

She responded, "You know. She's Nate's friend. Name is Dee."

"What's her story?" he asked.

"Calm down, Johnny boy." She laughed. "She's happily married. She and her husband are building their dream home. We're doing the construction loan."

Gumba shrugged his shoulders. Such trivial details would not get in the way of his desires.

Gumba, of course, took a keen interest in the progression of Dee's mortgage banking career. She could barely spell "processor" before he promoted her to loan officer. He informed her that the timing was good because a loan officer training course The Company used was starting up again. It would start in a week in Baltimore, MD, and The Company would, of course, provide room and board. Dee was most excited and thanked Johnny profusely. Gumba would make sure she had ample opportunity to express her gratitude.

The "room" was a luxurious condominium that Gumba rented out for the two weeks that Dee would supposedly be "in training." The only question was, training for what? Reverend knew firsthand. That was because Gumba had Reverend feeding and walking his dogs for the two weeks of evenings he spent in Baltimore City. Of course, he wanted to make sure the accommodations were suitable for his prize loan officer.

The word spread throughout The Company that Johnny had taken up with Dee. He was strutting around like a peacock with full plumage. Dee's husband was not enamored of the news. He continued to call her at work, hoping to get her back in the fold. Gumba got wind of it and was not pleased. The next time he called, Gumba grabbed the phone and barked, "Son, don't bother calling her again. You got nothing on me. The fuckin' game is over for you."

Or so Johnny thought. Shortly after that, Dee announced that she was with child. The only problem was she didn't know who the father was. The good news was that there were only two possibilities – Gumba and her husband. She had kept the lines of communication open by continuing to sleep with her husband even as she shared Gumba's bed. So confusing! More than once, Dee proclaimed, "I don't know what to do. I so much love them both." Translation – she loved the lifestyle Gumba provided courtesy of his cash cow, but apparently, Johnny drew the short straw when it came to the length of his manhood. Such that in future lighter moments Dee referred to him as "Shortie."

A subsequent paternity test revealed that Johnny Gumba was in fact the father. Dee's husband's disgust level finally rose to the point that he agreed to grant her a divorce. Gumba won! But did he?

Chapter 6

The Clown Prince of Mortgage Banking

The Bugeaters Mortgage Banker of the Year candidates enjoyed a banner year in 1989. Bow (pronounced Bo) arrived at The Company in September. He came from a small mortgage brokerage company that had difficulty closing loans – especially his – due in part to that company's methods of operation and overall philosophy as much as Bow's personal modus operandi, which would soon become legendary within The Company.

Bow earned his nickname upon entering the lobby of The Company on his first day of work. He had the misfortune of encountering Eddie the Pec and introduced himself to the Bugeaters' chairman.

"You look like you spent the last six months on a horse," Eddie noted. "Your bowlegs would put a cowboy to shame. We're gonna call you Bow."

Before joining the mortgage banking industry, Bow had honed his sales skills selling vacuum cleaners in Charlottesville, Virginia. Not an early riser, he would typically go door-to-door midday, where his most common potential customers were stay-at-home housewives.

Upon opening the door, he greeted each woman with, "Ma'am, are you busy? Are you cleaning? Or was you busy cleaning?"

Most of the ladies didn't know whether to laugh or cry. He would then throw some dirt on the floor and attempt to vacuum it up. Sometimes it worked – sometimes, it didn't. He may not have made much money at it, but on occasion, Bow would parlay the call into an afternoon delight. Apparently, to his benefit, the theory that men with big noses were also well-endowed bore some truth. No wonder some of his friends called him Secretariat.

Bow put his salesmanship and work ethic into play with The Company. He usually arrived around 11 a.m. and spent an hour BS-ing with the Bugeaters. It was then out to lunch with the boys – the venue had changed to L&N Seafood, where they served great biscuits. Then back to The Company, where Bow would print up 400 rate sheets for alleged distribution to local real estate offices. His rate sheets attracted considerable attention because they contained more graffiti than the side of a Brooklyn subway car.

For example, Bow would write, "Ask about our service!"

A realtor might respond, "So Bow, how is your service?"

Bow: "It's great!"

Realtor: "Thanks, Bow."

Huh? "Hot seller," "Great money," and "Ask about our underwriting" frequented these sheets as well. Did putting "Great money" under one particular loan product mean the others were not so great? Bow tried not to read too deeply into such things.

The loan processors enjoyed doctoring up his rate sheets from time to time. They would write, "Free microwave oven with all jumbo loans," and change his title from Senior Loan Officer to Junior Loan Officer. The realtors always got a kick out of that one. Of course, Bow did not pick up on the processors' hijinks, which continuously blindsided him.

Unfortunately, Bow's rate sheets rarely found their way to the inside of any real estate offices because he was only trying to impress and fool Johnny Gumba, who had taken over as branch manager. He would take the 400 sheets and stop by Johnny's office to make small talk on the way out the door. Gumba would see the sheets and think Bow was "going out on the street" making sales calls. Fortunately for Bow, Gumba had no reason to inspect the dumpster at the rear of the building. Had he done so each day, he would have regularly seen the 400 sheets floating around with all the other trash. Bow had no time for sales calls. He would spend his afternoons at the mall, a bowling alley, or a barroom. When the weather was nice, Bow would mix in some golf. He also knew his way around the so-called gentlemen's clubs of Washington, DC. He would often use a pay phone to inform a borrower how hard he was working to get their loan approved before he sat front and center of the main stage at Good Guys or Camelot. All the dancers knew him by name and reputation. He would always stop back by the office around the close of business and inform Gumba "how rough it is out there."

Bow was certainly an engaging character. Being from the South, he had an air of country elegance. His favorite greeting was, "Whatcha know good?" Depending upon who you talked to, Bow was either a great salesman or the biggest BS-er who ever walked the earth.

Despite what some thought, however, his loan origination volume was impressive. Those who mistakenly equated his rural ways and demeanor to a bumpkin often found themselves in for a rude awakening, for at the end of the day, Bow was a wolf in a forest of sheep – a shark in a sea of minnows.

Bow's best buddy at his previous employer, the broker shop, was Reverend, who had once attempted to impart his spirituality onto others, which was easy because he did look like a man of the cloth. Bow kept in touch with Reverend and informed him how impressed he was with Daddy and his operation because they were actually concerned with closing loans and doing so on time. What a revelation! Bow wanted Reverend to make the move to The Company, so Reverend finally agreed to an interview with Johnny Gumba. He recalled Gumba not being particularly excited about hiring him but reluctantly agreed to do so. He did inform Reverend that he would "keep an eye on him," which was consistent with Gumba's approach to business in general, fancying himself a Mafia Don, lording over his soldiers and followers.

Reverend posted up at The Company in November of 1989.

On Reverend's first day, Bow told him he needed a ride somewhere. Being grateful for Bow getting him over to The Company, Reverend felt compelled to accede to his wishes. Bow directed him, and they eventually pulled up to a VD clinic. Bow told him to wait in the car, and he would be right out. One shot later, and he was back in Reverend's vehicle. Being astute, Reverend surmised that Bow was keeping some questionable company.

After settling in and getting the lay of the land, Reverend thought he had died and gone to heaven. Outfitted with the best furniture and prints money could buy, Reverend's office was evidence that Daddy spared no expense. The originators all wore the most expensive suits available. The support staff, specifically the loan processors, included some of the best-looking women in town, which was, of course, Johnny Gumba's doing. As impressive as it all was, Reverend recalled how he had barely been able to support his growing family on his meager salary during the several years working for the federal government before coming to the mortgage industry. On average, he might perform about one hour of actual work each day while being bored silly, so Reverend was excited to be at The Company in his fancy office.

Bow was even more excited than Reverend that he was at The Company because, in essence, Reverend acted as Bow's assistant. The Bugeaters referred to him as Bow's valet. Reverend was good-natured about it. He drove Bow everywhere, ran errands, and attempted to keep him out of trouble as much as possible, which was a difficult task. The two were inseparable.

This dynamic duo amused the Bugeaters, who accepted them daily at their lunch table. Earl had taken a liking to Reverend – he found him to be a very decent human being.

Earl took issue with Reverend performing his valet duties. Earl liked Bow, too. However, along with the other Bugeaters, Earl could not comprehend how Bow could do the kind of volume that he did while indulging in his antics and maintaining his lifestyle. Even though they continually sought to question Reverend about this great mystery, he had nothing to offer. In his mind, Bow was the ultimate salesman who could produce a maximum amount of loan volume with a minimum amount of effort.

The support staff was not so complimentary of Bow, who routinely forgot about loan files until it was almost the closing date, sometimes the day before. If anyone asked about the status of a file, Bow would respond, "I'm just the loan officer. How would I know?" Upon recognizing a targeted settlement, he would grab the file and head to Daddy's office, hoping Daddy wasn't still hung over. Bow would fabricate some excuse why, once again, his loan was coming down to the last minute and explain that his best real estate agent had referred the loan. But Daddy had heard that one before. Every single time one of his loan officers got his tit in a wringer, it involved their "best agent." Inevitably, Daddy would waltz the file down to processing and demand the loan be closed on time. The processors and closers would drop what they were doing and miraculously perform the priority task. Of course, Bow claimed he was instrumental in getting it done each time, and after a few of these saves, he felt he had become a mortgage banking superhero. Bow was skating, and the ice was getting smoother every day.

The wasted rate sheet daily count reached 800 with Reverend contributing to the outdoor dumpster. The mall and the bowling alley gained favor in terms of where they spent their afternoons. Reverend was partial to the bowling alley because there was a real estate office across the street where he allegedly tried to solicit business. Johnny Gumba was particularly interested in that office, one of several from the same firm referring business to him and The Company. So, the benefit to Reverend was that if Johnny paged him, he could rush across the street to return the call. Gumba would think he was making sales calls instead of bowling a few lines. Reverend would also bring back some competitors' rate sheets, which pleased Johnny and further precipitated the ruse.

Earl got a big kick out of these two yahoos' daily routine. He asked them one day, "Has it ever occurred to you two that you are employed in a hundred percent commissioned business where, if you don't work, you don't get paid?" He never got an answer.

Bow summed up his mortgage banking and business philosophy in seven words: "An ignorant consumer is my best customer." The Washington Post published a real estate article every Saturday designed to educate people on all facets of the industry. Mortgage banking received a lot of the press, and much of it was less than favorable. Loan originators always read the articles to see what they might have to defend themselves against the following week. Bow always seemed able to conjure up some BS to counter any objections or questions from borrowers.

Then The Article came out. Even Bow froze like a weak hitter taking a 100-mph fastball.

Bow thought it might be a good time to take a vacation – a real long one.

However, Bow was able to dance around any fallout from The Article because he had always utilized a tactic not referenced in The Article. (At the end of this chapter.) His ace-in-the-hole card was "the loan committee." While typically used in commercial lending and sometimes in niche residential situations, The Company had no loan committee and would never have one. That did not deter Bow from informing many of his borrowers that their credit situation was dire, and that loan approval was in question. "Dire" would often be a one-time, thirty-day late payment on a credit card from more than three years earlier. Bow would explain that the loan must go before "the committee" for a final resolution. The good news was that as a top producer, Bow purported to be tight with "the committee" and was able to rescue many loans like this in the past. Naturally, the borrowers (victims) were extremely nervous, anxious – and grateful.

Bow would let things ride for a couple of days to increase their anxiety level even more and then inform them of the great news. They were approved! Of course, "the committee" determined that one point had to be added to the loan price to compensate for the credit situation. The borrowers were nevertheless pleased because they would get their new home. Bow and Johnny Gumba were pleased because the extra point would be split between Bow and The Company – clearly a win-win situation.

New Year's 1990 came and went, and suddenly, the spring market was in place again. Time flies when you're having fun! And the Bugeaters were having fun. Although Bow had been at The Company a relatively short time, he had become a dominant club figure. His antics and shenanigans were becoming legendary. He was fast approaching a Michael-Jordan-like status. His salesmanship and cunning were well-documented, but he proved an easy target for the Bugeaters' jokes and scams.

A prime example was Good Friday of Easter weekend. Earl was sitting in his office at 11 a.m. and was surprised to see Bow wandering down the hall toward Johnny's office with the obligatory 400 rate sheets. What was he doing here on a holiday weekend? Certainly not working.

"Hey, Bow," said Earl, "let me see what you're selling this weekend."

Bow handed over a sheet.

Earl reviewed it and said, "You don't get it, do you?"

Bow didn't understand.

"You're missing the point. What weekend is it?" asked Earl.

"It's Easter weekend," said Bow.

"Right. Right. Nobody in this business works on holiday weekends. So, you put 'will work Easter Sunday' on your rate sheet, and you are guaranteed to get every deal in this town!" cried Earl.

Bow was ecstatic. He dumped the 400 rate sheets in the waste can and headed back to his office. An hour later, he approached Earl with a new bumper crop of rate sheets. Emblazoned across the top in bold letters was "Will Work Easter Sunday."

"What the hell are you doing?" asked Earl.

Bow was confused. "What do you mean?"

"You can't do that. These realtors will think you're sacrilegious."

Bow looked like he saw a ghost. He threw the sheets in the trash and ran out of the building. Earl could not stop laughing. He had some more Bow fodder for the Bugeaters.

Despite Bow's shortcomings, he had cultivated a sizable group of realtors who referred business to him. One such person was a successful woman who always wore fancy hats like she was dressed up and ready to go to church. She published an impressive monthly newsletter and somehow came up with the idea of having the Clown Prince write articles on mortgage banking. Bow proved he could plagiarize with the best of them. One such article he copied referenced the Persian Gulf crisis and underlying market fundamentals and technicals. If asked, Bow probably thought the Persian Gulf crisis referred to an oil well fire. He clearly had no clue about market fundamentals and technicals. But who cared? It made for good copy. The lady in the fancy hat was happy and continued to refer business to him, despite Bow being Bow.

Eddie attended a real estate conference at Northern Virginia Community College twenty years later. When he entered the large conference hall and mingled through the crowd, he saw a lady sitting at a table sporting a wide-brimmed, stylish hat. It was she! He approached her and introduced himself. They made small talk.

Then Eddie said, "Many years ago, I had the pleasure of working with Bow. Do you remember him?"

She smiled and said, "He's a rascal!"

That he was.

Mortgage shoppers must be wary of application scams

Washington, D.C.
Home buyers and refinancers shopping for the most competitive mortgage rates should be on guard against this summer's bumper crop of loan application scams: Low-ball quotes that evaporate on paper, bait-and-switch ploys, and "no-cost" cream-puff deals that can be far costlier than ordinary mortgages.

Here's a quick overview of some of the latest scams, based on interviews with lenders and mortgage brokers active in major markets across the United States.

Low-balling

This is most frequently found in metropolitan areas where borrowers have a wide choice of competing lenders, and often do their initial rate-shopping by phone. It's also commonplace where local newspapers or real-estate publications print weekly selections of loan quotes by local lending firms.

When a prospective borrower phones for rates and terms, according to industry sources, the low-baller deliberately offers a quote that's a notch below anybody else's in the market. What the lender doesn't mention is that the rate is only guaranteed or "locked" for 10 days. After that it floats to whatever level the lender wants.

In other words, if you were able to close on your new mortgage or refinancing within 10 days, you could indeed get the cut-rate deal you were quoted. But who's prepared to complete an appraisal, credit check, title search and all the legal paperwork in 10 days on a home loan? Virtually nobody.

And when do you typically find out that the rate you were quoted by phone was a 10-day wonder? At best, say loan executives, when you come to the mortgage company office and you're well along into the formal application process.

But some borrowers, particularly refinancers, don't hear about the evaporating rate-lock until much closer to settlement date. The 7.5 percent, 30-year loan they thought they were getting has now turned into an 8 percent loan, or higher. Refinancers are especially vulnerable because a loophole in existing federal law allows lenders to withhold truth-in-lending "good

Nation's housing
Kenneth Harney

faith estimate" disclosures until settlement.

Diane Kelly, president of the 1,700-member National Association of Mortgage Brokers, says low-balling is "unquestionably a problem" that the mortgage industry needs to control. Consumers can avoid being snared, she said, by asking any provider of loan quotes — over the phone or face to face — one basic question: How long is your quote good for?

Many lenders offer rate packages that can be locked for 60 days, 45 days, 30 days or 10 to 12 days, Kelly said. To truly compare apples with apples, or anges with oranges, "you've got to ask how long the rate is actually protected." If the rate or fees could go up sharply by tomorrow morning, what good is today's low quote?

Bait and switch

Often used in tandem with low-balling, bait-and-switch techniques "can be so slickly done that the (victim) doesn't even know anything happened," according to a mortgage executive with a national firm. The "bait" may be a low-rate, no-points, no-closing-costs refinancing package, for instance. The quote may be made over the phone or across a desk. What isn't revealed up front, however, is that the package is reserved solely for borrowers with immaculate credit — not even the tiniest late-payment blemish on a charge card is allowed.

The applicant puts up a standard $300 to $375 nonrefundable deposit to cover credit-check and appraisal costs. In some cases, the nonrefundable application fee totals ½ to 1 percent of the mortgage amount. Two weeks later the loan officer re-

ports back that "I'm sorry, you've got this late payment on your credit history. Now of course, we know you're a good credit risk, but our (funding source) insists on absolute perfection. So let me tell you what we can do for you. . . ."

Then the loan officer steers the borrower into a higher-cost loan package than the original. "Properly done," said one Baltimore area lender who claims to have watched colleagues conduct bait-and-switch transactions, "it's an art form. Of course, it's also basically illegal."

No closing costs, no points

Refinancers need to look hard and long at loan packages when the lender claims he's paying all closing costs and charging no "points." A point is equal to 1 percent of the loan amount. Mortgage industry executives say no-closing-cost packages are not necessarily rip-offs, but they may be financially less attractive than they first appear.

No-points, no-closing-cost mortgages always come with a higher interest rate. In a market where standard 30-year fixed-rate loans go for 8 percent with 2 points, no-closing-cost loans may be quoted at 8.5 to 8.75 percent.

What isn't disclosed to the borrower is that the loan originators may be getting $3,000 to $3,500 in extra premiums and fees from investors who buy the higher-rate loans from them. The borrower often ends up paying an excessively-high monthly mortgage rate for years, "saves" nothing, and merely improves the loan originator's bottom line.

Distributed by the Washington Post Writers Group. Kenneth Harney is a nationally syndicated columnist. He can be contacted at Box 4038, Chevy Chase, Md. 20815.

McClintock

Continued from page 1R

contractors questions viewers might ask without offering construction expertise. Nuts-and-bolts information may come from an inarticulate, camera-shy electrician summed up by a host who doesn't know the subject. I sometimes just give up on the narra-

THE NATION'S HOUSING

NO POINTS!! NO CLOSING COSTS! LOWEST RATES IN TOWN!!
FLEECE MORTGAGE REFINANCING
FOR QUALIFIED CUSTOMERS

BY WILLIAM T. COULTER

Beware of Hidden Costs In a Deal Too Good to Be True

HARNEY, From E1

packages when the lender claims he's paying all closing costs and charging no points. A point equals 1 percent of the loan amount. Industry executives say no-closing-cost packages are not necessarily rip-offs, but they may be financially less attractive than they first appear.

No-points, no-closing-cost mortgages always come with a higher interest rate. In a market where standard 30-year fixed-rate loans go for 8 percent with two points, no-closing-cost loans may be quoted at 8.5 percent to 8.75 percent.

What isn't disclosed to the borrower is that the loan originators may be getting $3,000 to $3,500 in extra premiums and fees from investors who buy the higher-rate loans from them. The borrower often pays an excessively high monthly mortgage rate for years, saves nothing and merely improves the loan originator's bottom line.

Chapter 7

Bow's Lackey

Perhaps the best way to describe and sum up the life and times of Johnny Gumba's younger brother, Tim, is to invoke some lyrics from "Truckin'" by the *Grateful Dead* – their most famous song: "What a long, strange trip it's been."

Tim's real name was what one might imagine it to be – vintage Italian like something out of *The Godfather*. Why Tim? Because when he first showed up at The Company in 1991, Reverend suggested that the Bugeaters ask Tim to lunch.

"Who the hell is Tim?" asked Earl.

"You know," answered Reverend. "Gumba's little brother."

Earl, who is half-Italian, was beside himself.

"Are you joking? You think that WOP's name is Tim? Okay, Tim it is," said Earl as he shook his head and laughed.

Tim took a very circuitous route to The Company. He finished college in West Virginia, where his family was from, and then attended law school in Texas. After graduation, he became a public defender in a mid-sized town in the Lone Star State. His life took a 180-degree turn when he was assigned to represent a woman jailed on an insurance fraud allegation. Tim arrived at the jail to meet his client and discovered she was incredibly sexy and good-looking. She had, in fact, at one time graced the stages of some of the local gentlemen's clubs. Within a day, Tim arranged for bail and had his client back out on the street, so to speak. He immediately purchased two plane tickets to Las Vegas for himself and his newfound friend. They flew in, found a nearby chapel, and got hitched.

Clearly a match made in heaven.

Meanwhile, big brother Johnny was knockin' 'em dead at The Company. The huge early-'90s refinance boom was in place, and the loan originators and The Company were making money hand over fist. In addition to the Machiavellian approach Gumba took to business was his fondness for nepotism. Over time, he stocked The Company with family and friends. Although he maintained a love-hate relationship with Tim, Gumba convinced Tim to make the move to Northern Virginia to share in the spoils of the fruitful mortgage banking business. Gumba's action was sincere and well-intended but would someday prove to be the worst decision he ever made.

Tim showed up at The Company ready to take on the mortgage-lending world and originate some loans. How ready was he? This attorney traveled halfway across the country to sign up for a one-hundred-percent-commissioned job that he had neither experience in nor knowledge of.

Tim took a curious approach on his first day on the job. His first mistake was befriending Bow and going to lunch with him. His second mistake was accompanying Bow that afternoon on another whirlwind tour of the DC strip clubs.

The Bugeaters were loving this, especially when Johnny Gumba got wind of it and proceeded to tear Tim a new one.

Tim was clearly not fazed by the verbal beating from his brother. Not one bit. This was evident one week later when he got his first deal and the borrowers showed up for the loan application. Tim was AWOL. Earl had to meet with the clients to keep them in tow. The Bugeaters posted heavy odds that Tim was back downtown with Bow on the strip joint circuit. There were no takers.

Earl was beginning to realize that this phenomenon was beyond anything the Bugeaters had experienced in their four years of existence. Tim had the potential to dominate the annual awards for years to come.

Tim's arrival proved to be a godsend for Reverend. Why? Because Tim became Bow's de facto valet, freeing up Reverend. He assumed the daily driving responsibilities and errand running. Tim followed Bow around like a loyal puppy dog. Bow was clearly not the best choice for a role model. Of course, Tim was present for the daily excursions to the mall and bowling alley. And he was more than happy to contribute to the wasted rate sheet daily count.

For some reason, Tim referred to Reverend as Preacher Man. Every morning, he would show up at The Company and ask, "What is your plan, Preacher Man?"

Reverend generally had no response and would let Bow answer for him.

The dynamic duo had become the terrific trio.

Just as the Bugeaters' favorite whipping boy was Ab La Sword, Johnny Gumba's was Tim.

Gumba berated his brother mercilessly daily, generally in front of an audience, which went way beyond Tim's tenure at The Company. It had been going on his entire life: big brother dominating little brother.

Once again, the Bugeaters had a new sideshow for their viewing, listening, and lunchtime pleasure. Tim seemed somewhat immune to it all. Whenever Gumba verbally lashed out at him, Tim would smile and move on. He would usually seek out his mentor Bow and head to wherever that day's adventure was waiting.

Every Monday morning, Gumba held court at the weekly loan officer meeting. All of the loan officers wondered what time the 9:00

a.m. meeting would start, which basically depended on Gumba's servicing schedule that morning. The highlight of Gumba's week was having all of his moneymakers in the same room at the same time under his control. He was in his glory and referred to this event as his "cash cow." Topics ranged from production numbers to new product guidelines to industry news.

Attending his first loan officer meeting was an eye-opener for Tim. Halfway through the session, Tim raised his hand and began to ask a question about some procedures.

Gumba was incensed. Interrupting Tim mid-question, he banged his fist on the table and, at the top of his voice, cried, "Rookies don't ask questions at loan officer meetings!"

Say what? Who should ask questions? If there was any doubt about where Tim stood in Johnny Gumba's world, Gumba clearly defined it at that moment.

Despite the wrath that Gumba constantly vented at Tim, he still felt responsible for seeing that his younger brother made a decent living. So, Gumba assigned Tim to originate loans for one of the prime builder projects, virtually guaranteed business. Due to Daddy's diligence and connections in the builder community, The Company remained the prevalent lender for area builders. Loan officers assigned to a builder were basically order-takers. Even so, one had to provide good service to borrowers and builder reps alike while making sure the loans went to settlement on time.

Although Gumba rode herd on these loans, it did not go well. Borrowers complained to the builder, who, in turn, complained to Daddy. Perhaps Tim was too busy functioning as Bow's valet to service the project properly. Maybe it was simply Tim being Tim. In any event, Gumba pulled the project from Tim and awarded it to Eddie the Pec, who got the majority of the loans settled and made a nice buck doing it. At least Tim was consistent; he continued to wear out his welcome.

The Bugeaters began to realize why Tim stuck around and incurred the wrath of his big brother – he existed in a fantasy world. What made Tim dangerous was that he didn't know he was dangerous. Even Bow, as big of a BS-er as was hanging around Northern Virginia, knew his limitations. He realized he was only as good as the people who surrounded him. He could keep skating as long as he didn't tick them off too much and too often. Of course, drinking with Daddy every day was critical to Bow's survival. Tim didn't have that luxury. Daddy thought he was a flake and tolerated him only because he was Gumba's brother.

Tim floored Reverend one day when he informed him that he could go to another mortgage banking firm and bring a large percentage of The Company's employees with him if he wanted to. Tim would lead them to the Promised Land.

What was he smoking?

Then came the Atlantic City trip. Columbo, one of the original Bugeaters, lined up a three-day boondoggle featuring gambling, renting a fishing boat, and the obligatory heavy drinking.

Immediately prior to the trip, B.B. signed up with The Company. He came from Iowa, and his father was one of Daddy's best friends. B.B. wasn't exactly setting the world on fire, so Daddy convinced him to come to Northern Virginia to seek fame and fortune. B.B.'s previous claim to fame was surviving a three-story fall from a Cancun hotel balcony and landing on his head during spring break. Nobody quite knew if some extreme willpower pulled him through, or perhaps it was the tequila-induced haze he floated around in for that week.

Bow immediately recognized B.B.'s potential and took him under his wing. This new protégé would make a fine valet if Tim ever flamed out. Once again, Bow was one step ahead of the game.

The Bugeaters were to travel by train to Atlantic City, which left Union Station at 1 p.m., so Bow gathered up his two lackeys, Tim and B.B., and arrived at 10 a.m., which allowed for a solid three hours of drinking before the train departed. The rest of the group arrived just prior to departure. The estimated arrival time was 5 p.m., and the usual card game commenced immediately in the train car. The drink of choice was Johnny Walker Black. Columbo plunked a fresh bottle down on the table. The players became continually more boisterous as the game wore on, plied by the straight scotch they gulped, much to the amusement (or consternation) of the many non-Bugeaters in the train car.

The appraiser The Company sent business to, Barry Seeless, should have been honored to be the only non-Bugeater invited on the trip. Instead, he unceremoniously won all of the money. Further, he didn't even offer to buy a round once the game finished up. Earl was not pleased and made a mental note that "Seelees will get his."

It was now 4 p.m. with ETA around one hour. The whole group was drunk as a bunch of monkeys, with B.B. topping the list. Earl thought it was appropriate to inform B.B. that it was time for his acceptance speech into the Bugeaters.

B.B. staggered to the middle of the train car and proceeded to mumble unintelligibly, "I love the Bugeaters. I love the Bugeaters. I love you guys. You're the best thing to ever happen to me. I love you. I –"

Earl couldn't take any more. He ushered B.B. to his seat. Every person in the train car, many laughing so hard they had tears in their eyes, stood up and gave B.B. and the Bugeaters a standing ovation. It was good to be alive and in the club.

What was at once a glorious moment for B.B. turned quickly south. Upon arrival, the group exited the train to a line of taxicabs waiting to take them to the hotel three miles away. Earl hailed a cab for B.B., Columbo, and himself. The cabbie grabbed the bags and threw them in the trunk. As Earl started to get into the front seat, he turned to check on B.B. and almost went into shock. B.B. had closed the back door on his own hand, but he was so blotto he didn't realize it. He hadn't made a sound. Earl pulled B.B.'s hand out, and sat him down in the back seat.

He and Columbo agreed this was going to be one hell of a trip.

It got worse. Standing in the check-in line at the hotel, B.B. asked Earl to watch his bags. B.B. made his way to a craps table and proceeded to lose $500 before he could even check in at the front desk. After check-in, the Bugeaters met – where else? – in the hotel bar. B.B. continued to throw gasoline on the fire.

Later on, Earl decided to call it a night because they had an 8 a.m. start at the fishing boat. As he exited the bar, Earl noticed B.B. chatting up a shapely blonde. Earl laughed to himself, thinking that even if she were up for it, B.B. would have the worst case of whiskey dick (some might say brewer's droop) known to mankind.

B.B. had a very different thought process, however. He was most impressed by how friendly and outgoing these East Coast women were. She even suggested they make their way up to his room! He agreed, and after fumbling with his keys for several minutes, he could enter the room.

Before he could mumble anything else, she looked at him and said, "Okay, hotshot, have you figured out how you're going to pay for this?"

Fortunately for B.B., he passed out before he could process her request.

But he wasn't done for the night. Around 2 a.m., Earl was awakened from a deep sleep by a phone call from Barry Seeless.

"Earl, I need your help."

Earl was not happy. "With what?"

"I'm rooming with B.B., and he puked on my bags. What should I do?"

"Puke on his bags," Earl growled as he hung up the phone. What would tomorrow bring?

Somehow, the Bugeaters made it to the boat by 8 a.m., and the good news was that nobody was hungover. The bad news was they were all still drunk from the day before – nothing that a round of Bloody Marys couldn't solve. Captain Jack fired up the boat stereo with some live Stones, and off they went. The captain had been working on the water for over fifty years and was more than content to stay away from these yahoos and remain in the captain's tower. He would let the deckhand deal with them.

By 11 a.m., the whole group was well-tuned-up. Tim, who had spent his entire life in the landlocked state of West Virginia, was not adapting well to being twenty miles off the coast, bouncing around in the five-foot swells. He began to upchuck off the side of the boat, donating his dinner and breakfast to any unfortunate fish nearby. The Bugeaters were pleased that Tim was chumming the waters; they had not so much as had a bite.

Earl couldn't help himself and went over to Tim to inform him that his brother was on the phone.

Tim cried, "Johnny's on the phone? Where?"

Earl pointed upward and replied, "On Captain Jack's line."

Tim, sick as a dog, raced up the ladder and confronted the good captain who had been enjoying the privacy of his tower cabin, peacefully smoking his pipe as he piloted his boat.

Tim screamed at the top of his lungs, "Give me your phone! John's looking for me!"

Captain Jack was not amused, noting Tim's ashen face, hair standing up like a porcupine, and vomit clinging to his unshaven chin.

"Ya listen to me, and ya listen to me good, sonny boy," he snarled. "Ya take ya arse back down that fuckin' ladder and go feed some more fish. I'm done with ya."

Tim put his tail between his legs and scampered back down the ladder, much to the delight of the Bugeaters. He still had five more hours to endure on that godforsaken boat.

To nobody's surprise, not one fish was caught. But that wasn't the point. They were out on the water with good tunes, good drink, and good company. The boat pulled into the dock at 4 p.m., and the Bugeaters headed back to the hotel. They were all three sheets to the wind.

Earl went upstairs and went to bed. After two solid days of drinking, he needed some rest. At 7 p.m., he was, once again, rudely awakened by a phone call, this time from the hotel bar manager demanding that he come downstairs and take control of Big Marvin, who was off the charts.

Earl felt like a glorified babysitter but was well aware of Marvin's propensity to tie on a big one. He also figured the manager might be intimidated; Marvin was six-foot-five and close to three bills. Earl reported to the gin mill to find Marvin's eyes rolling around in the back of his head – after drinking close to a case of beer and every known form of liquor, Marvin had decided to top it off with a nice bottle of red. Earl was able to coax him out of the bar and into the elevator. He got him upstairs and pushed him into his room. Earl retired once again.

The Bugeaters traveled back to Northern Virginia the next day without incident. They were too wasted to do anything but sleep on the train. Nobody was arrested, so they considered the trip a success. Bow was pleased that his new understudy B.B. had made his bones on the trip. Of course, Johnny Gumba berated Tim for making an ass out of himself. Tim expected nothing less, and that's what he got.

Tim's next travel was on official company business – the 1993 President's Club trip to Naples, Florida. You made the trip if you did a certain level of business, which in those busy times was easily attainable. All the Bugeaters made it except Ab La Sword – a story for another day. Tim was pretty proud of himself; he strutted around like a rooster the whole time. Eddie was annoyed and began to refer to Tim as "the cockroach." Tim did his best to ignore him until the wrap-up dinner when the mariachi band hired as the evening's entertainment came to his table and serenaded him with "La Cuckaracha." Eddie put them up to it, of course.

One month later, Eddie was dining at The Palm restaurant in Washington, DC, when a short Italian lady approached his table and grabbed him by the shirt. It was Tim's mother. She barked, "The next time you call my son a cockroach, you're gonna get your ass kicked," convincing Eddie she wasn't joking.

At long last, the combination of Johnny Gumba berating him and the Bugeaters riding him drove Tim to submit his resignation. Earl helped him clean out his office and carried his monstrous IBM computer to his car. Tim cancelled his resignation the next day and showed up at the office. Earl carried his computer back in. Tim repeated this process once a week for the next three weeks. He simply changed the date on his resignation letter and resubmitted it to Gumba.

Earl wondered why he maintained his gym membership; he was getting all the exercise he needed carrying Tim's computer back and forth. It didn't look like it then, but Tim would eventually get the last laugh.

Chapter 8

The Whipping Boy

Every locker room, frat house, and club have a whipping boy. The Bugeaters' was the one and only Ab La Sword.

Ab was a nerd, a geek – and a mama's boy to boot. A great combination. He had somehow incurred the ire of the head Bugeater, Eddie the Pec, who had a big-time hard-on for Ab and wouldn't let it go. It may have been because before then, Eddie was financing a real estate transaction on which La Sword's mother was the listing agent. For forty-five days and nights, she badgered Eddie incessantly. The loan finally closed, and Eddie felt like the world had been lifted from his shoulders. But he did not forget the harassment. Or maybe Eddie just didn't care for nerds.

Regardless, he used every opportunity available to make Ab's life miserable.

Of course, Ab brought most of this on himself. He certainly did not endear himself to the membership when, at his first lunch, he whipped out a tip calculator when it was time to pay. Since many of the Bugeaters fancied themselves as big swinging dicks, this antic went over like a lead balloon. Mr. Miller had worked with Ab at some previous lenders' shops and considered him a friend. However, this relationship with one of the founding fathers of the Bugeaters was not enough to save him. Ab was simply too easy a target. Just as the processing staff loved to doctor up Bow's rate sheets, the Bugeaters also went after La Sword's. Noting that he jumped from lender to lender several times, they would print at the bottom of his sheets, *"Let me put my experience to work for you. I've been with eight companies in the past three years."* Naturally, the realtors he attempted to solicit business from were real excited to see that.

Ab was a sharp dresser. Eddie probably disliked that, too. Monogrammed shirts, cufflinks, and gold tie clasps were the order of the day for Ab. He would roll up daily to The Company in his little Beemer, which his mother had bought for him, and begin his routine comparing The Company's rates to every lender in the area. A local newspaper that published approximately fifty lenders' rate quotes daily was the basis for comparison. Ab would go line by line and note the spread between The Company's rates and the competition. Regardless of the results, La Sword would complain that The Company was out of the market, precluding him from getting any business. La Sword performed his daily routine for two reasons: he needed an excuse for not bringing in any business, and since he had no loans, he had nothing else to do.

Word eventually reached Daddy that Mister La Sword was not particularly enamored with his pricing policy. Daddy was not pleased. Why he let it ride for a while remained to be seen. It may have had something to do with Ab's wife being The Company's head underwriter.

Ab and the Missus were clearly an odd couple. Having logged several years in the Northern Virginia mortgage banking arena, Ab's wife was no stranger to the party scene that engulfed it. The word around was that she had dated some gentlemen of – to be kind – dubious distinction. Perhaps she had settled on Ab as some type of atonement. Or maybe she merely wanted someone she could easily dominate. Lyrics from an old Rolling Stones tune come to mind: *"Now she's here and there, with every man in town, still trying to take me for that same old clown."* And dominate, she did. Eddie was extremely amused to find out that as a prerequisite to getting home for dinner on time, she forced Ab to return home in the afternoon and thoroughly clean the house. He wasn't working anyway, and it was a vain attempt to keep him out of several DC strip clubs he frequented because he was not getting it at home. However, the Bugeaters were convinced that Ab couldn't get laid in a women's prison, even if he tried!

Ab's lack of business along with constant complaints was wearing thin on Daddy. The Bugeaters were aware of this situation (they didn't miss much) and sought to take advantage of it. So, it was received with great joy when a well-read metro DC magazine featured a photograph of Ab sitting on a barstool in a popular local nightspot. The Bugeaters altered the photo by placing a clock on the wall reading 3 p.m. and adding this dialogue balloon flowing from the barmaid's lips: *"Ab, you've already had the burger deluxe twice this week. Why don't you try the special today?"* Somehow, a copy of the photo found its way into Daddy's inbox. To say that he was not amused was an understatement. Ab was skating on thinner ice every day.

Earl wasn't as eager to bust La Sword's chops as Eddie was, but he couldn't help himself at times. For example, a great idea dawned on Earl one day when he made a sales call on an Alexandria real estate office he was trying to break into. Every time Earl entered the office, the same realtor cornered him, demanding to know his progress on getting approval for a condominium project she marketed. Even though Earl was tired of it, he didn't want to just blow her off. The condo was not approvable because almost one hundred percent of its occupants were renters, and lenders typically wanted to see sixty percent of the occupants be owners. Earl dreaded addressing this impasse with her again – then the light bulb clicked on.

"I have some good news for you today," said Earl, brightening. "The Company has hired a condominium specialist to deal with these issues. He's sharp as a tack. His name is Ab La Sword. If anybody can make this happen, it's Ab. I'll put him in touch with you."

Earl went back to the office and asked Missy, the receptionist, to write up a phone message for Ab with the realtor's name and phone number on it. He told Missy to make sure that she informed him that the realtor had a loan to refer. Ab called her immediately, and she roped him in. Earl was thankfully off the hook. The realtor attached herself to Ab for his remaining days at The Company. Such was the price of fame.

Interest rates dropped dramatically in the early '90s, precipitating a refinance boom. There was almost too much business to handle, and it was tough to keep up. Originators doing a certain level of business qualified for The Company's President's Club and were rewarded with a vacation to a tropical resort. In that kind of market, attaining the necessary volume to make the trip was easy. Even then, Ab didn't qualify. Maybe he didn't care. But he was not happy to receive a postcard from Eddie that read, *"Greetings from Naples, Fla. Wish you could be here."*

At times, the volume was such that the originators would like to turn off the spigot. Earl came back from lunch one day and had ten phone messages to return. He went to his office, and the phone rang. He picked up.

"This is Earl."

A redneck-sounding voice said, "Be lookin' to get me a ree-fy-nantz."

Earl was not thrilled.

"Is that so? Where is your property, sir?" he asked wearily.

"Hayid Kinnie Mer-lin" was the response.

"Ah, would that be Howard County, Maryland?"

"Day-am straight. Y'all got a funny accent, too. Where ya from, boy?"

"Boston, Mass."

"Thought so. Nice town."

"You've been there?"

"No."

Earl could hardly take any more. His mind floated to the three closings he had going that afternoon. "Please give me some details on your situation," he requested.

"Well, me and the ol' lady got us an ee-fish-ancee con-doh-mineeum. Helluvanice buildin'. The tenant's okay most times. Don't like his dawg much, though. It's worth all of fifty thousand. Want to borrow thirty."

Earl wanted to light his hair on fire. An investment condo in Howard County, Maryland, on which this *jabroni* wants to borrow $30K? Earl took control. "Sir, you've come to the right place. We have here at The Company a condo specialist who likes to focus on rental properties. He does a lot of business up your way. His name is Ab La Sword. I am going to transfer you over to him. Make sure you mention my name."

The customer finished up with, "Much obliged, Earl. You're a good man."

La Sword was in Earl's doorway in less than five minutes. His forehead, on which he had a widow's peak, was fire-engine red, and his veins were popping like firecrackers.

He screamed at the top of his lungs, "You need to stop this."

Cool as a cucumber, Earl said, "Just helpin' out, brother. Business is business."

Ab continued to be Ab. Just as Daddy was pretty much at the end of his rope with him, so was Johnny Gumba, who was always on Ab to get out on the street and bring in some loans. One afternoon, Eddie and Earl were in Gumba's office chewing the fat. It was around 3 p.m., and Gumba was distracted with several issues. He mentioned something about La Sword and the need to get hold of him.

Eddie said, "If you want to reach him, call him at home."

Johnny answered, "He's not at home at this time."

"The hell he's not," cried Eddie. "He's there cleaning the house. Call him. Here's the number."

Johnny was skeptical but dialed the number and put it on speaker.

"Hello," said Ab.

Gumba went into an expletive-filled tirade that lasted three minutes. Ab tried to explain that he was at home having lunch, but Earl passed a note to Johnny stating that Ab had lunch with the Bugeaters two hours earlier. That wasn't true, but Gumba didn't need to know that.

Ab simply could not win.

Eddie had been lying in the weeds waiting to really nail La Sword with the right opportunity. It came the day that Ab let it be known that a conservative elderly couple was coming in that evening for a refinance loan application.

The folks arrived at 6:30 p.m., and a beaming La Sword ushered them in. He was happy to have any customers. The couple took seats in front of his desk and chatted a bit. Ab then explained that The Company had some mighty fancy desks with a pullout writing tablet they could utilize when it came time to sign the loan documents. Ab finished the application and handed the documents to the borrowers for their signatures. The gentleman pulled out the writing tablet as Ab suggested and let out a sound resembling a wounded animal. Abruptly, the couple stood up and let La Sword know how disgusted they were as they exited his office. Ab stood up and looked down at the protruding tablet. Taped to it was the full-page pullout of the Penthouse Pet of the Month – naked as the day she was born. Ab made a feeble attempt to yell down the hall, "This isn't my office!" but to no avail, especially since the couple had commented on what a good-looking family he had as they admired the pictures on his credenza.

The Bugeaters had struck again.

A day soon thereafter proved to be doomsday for Ab at The Company. He was walking out of the men's room at 10:30 a.m. when Daddy walked in nursing a major-league hangover.

Daddy was working on about three hours of sleep, and he muttered, "Mornin', Ab."

On his way out, Ab replied, "Your pricing sucks."

One hour later, Ab was looking for his ninth company in three years.

More importantly, the Bugeaters lost their favorite whipping boy.

Chapter 9

Riding the Gravy Train

"And did we tell you the name of the game, boy?
We call it riding the gravy train."
"Have a Cigar" – Pink Floyd, 1975 – *Wish You Were Here*

The Pink Floyd song was about music industry executives ripping off bands and living off the spoils. The Company gravy train represented a more amicable relationship between giver (Daddy) and recipients (employee parasites). The expression "feeding at the trough" comes to mind. The Company's train had many seats, and Daddy had no trouble keeping them filled. What seemed to evolve frequently was who was wearing the engineer's hat and who occupied the caboose. But all in all, they were all just bricks in the wall.

The main prerequisite for a seat on the train was the ability to drink large quantities of alcohol consistently for extended periods, from two in the afternoon to two in the morning, five days a week. Riders had most weekends off to spend some time with their families. Spouses or significant others tended not to complain too much – they were accustomed to lavish lifestyles. So, in essence, they were riding the train as well. Who said opposites attract?

The venue of Daddy's choice would remain the same until he became dissatisfied with something. For several years it was Artie's – a well-known Fairfax watering hole. Over time, Daddy spent thousands of dollars there, including the lavish tips he bestowed upon the help. Then one night, after several hours of imbibing, Daddy asked the manager on duty to let him take a sizable amount of cash off his company credit card. He apparently wanted to tip in cash that night. The manager refused his request and lived to regret it. Daddy paid his tab and moved the troops down the street to the nearest gin mill. He never set foot in Artie's again.

As noted, the cast of gravy train riders was a diverse group who individually remained in favor for varying amounts of time. By far, the character with the longest ride had a most curious moniker – Wall Street Joe. He was a country bumpkin who hailed from West Virginia and spent his days (including so-called work hours) reading *Field and Stream* and *Outdoor Life*. As in many cases, Joe had met Daddy in some Northern Virginia drinking establishment where he impressed him with his durability and ability to consume large amounts of alcohol. He lasted more than thirty years sucking The Company tit. And after all that time, nobody seemed to know what Wall Street Joe was supposed to be doing, including Joe himself.

Joe started with The Company as a loan originator back when Daddy was first getting started. He took an unconventional approach to his production. Once he reached one million dollars in any given month, he would stop originating until the beginning of the following month because more loans meant more problems and stress. Of course, this approach limited his income somewhat, but Joe was okay with that. He was a single guy who made enough to support his extensive drinking habit, amongst other vices. Daddy always picked up the tab, contributing to Joe's strategy of not overextending himself. After all, quality of life ruled.

In 1989, when Daddy moved The Company to the new location, he decided to set up a wholesale operation. The Company would provide money to mortgage brokers who needed funds. Like all aspects of mortgage banking, wholesaling could be a lucrative supplement to the larger retail operation. But like any department, it would only be as good as the people who staffed it. So, when Wall Street Joe and Mr. Z staffed the new wholesale department, it was not unusual to see a few eyebrows raised.

If Joe was the chief engineer on the gravy train, Mr. Z was right behind him. His relationship with Daddy went back to their days in St. Louis when they got started in the mortgage banking business. Mr. Z made the move to Northern Virginia with Daddy and eventually rode the train almost as long as Wall Street Joe.

Once they got established in Virginia, Mr. Z bought a house in the country with acreage and a large pond. Daddy showed up one day with a truck outfitted with a huge water tank filled with blue gill. He rolled it up to the edge and stocked the pond. It was a typically generous gesture on Daddy's part, and it also provided him with a favorite spot for when he wanted to do some fishing.

Years later, Mr. Z decided to sell the house and downsize. Reverend was at home on a Tuesday morning when the phone rang. Reverend's wife answered the phone, then nervously announced that it was Daddy. He picked up and Daddy greeted him with, "Morning. You working today?" Before Reverend could answer, Daddy barked, "Didn't think so. Grab your fishing pole. I'll pick you up in a half hour."

Daddy rolled up in the tank truck and picked up Reverend, who asked where they were going. Daddy said, "I'm gonna get my blue gill back." They went out to Mr. Z's property, where they spent the day fishing and drinking Coors Light. They placed all the fish caught in the tank on the truck. Daddy had since bought a house and property with a pond into which he transferred all the blue gill. All in a day's work!

The newly-established wholesale department was not exactly blowing up the bottom line. Wall Street Joe did not appear to be overly concerned. He spent his days perusing his many hunting and fishing magazines in the spacious, extravagantly decorated office Daddy had provided him, located on the first floor across from underwriting.

One day, Earl headed downstairs to underwriting to discuss one of his cases. Daddy was standing in the doorway to Wall Street Joe's office. When Daddy saw Earl, he cried out, "Earl. Come on over here."

Earl sauntered over, wondering what it was all about.

Daddy said, "Come in here. Take a look around. What do you think of this brand-new cherry wood furniture?"

Feeling uneasy, Earl said, "It's real nice. Very impressive."

"You think so?" asked Daddy. "What do you think, Joe? What do you think about the fact that Earl here did fourteen million for us last year and is on track to do more this year? He doesn't have furniture like this. You haven't done squat since we started this thing nine months ago. What the hell have you been doing?"

Joe's face was beet red.

Earl was embarrassed and did not want to be there.

Joe finally mumbled, "I've been working on these manuals."

"Horseshit!" yelled Daddy. "Get off your ass and get some business in here."

Such was the cost of riding the train.

Daddy laid it out pretty well during one of the countless gin-soaked evenings at Artie's. Mid-stream in some ridiculous discussion and in front of his full court, Daddy informed Wall Street Joe, "Always remember, m…er f…er, I pay you to be my friend."

Wall Street Joe figured it was about time to do something productive, or he might not be riding the gravy train much longer. So, he arranged to sign up a loan product for The Company that was the worst consumer product in the history of mortgage banking. It was an ARM, which was adjusted monthly with negative amortization. The way negative amortization worked was that the consumer could make an artificially low payment. The problem was adding the difference between the low and "real" payments to the loan balance. So, in essence, one would be going backward. Over time, the borrower would be way underwater. That didn't seem to faze Wall Street Joe, who advertised that with this product, "you control your own destiny." Indeed, your destiny could be foreclosure and possibly bankruptcy.

Although most gravy train riders utilized the popular approach to job security by being one of Daddy's bootlickers, some other avenues proved successful. While the good Reverend was not much of a drinker, automatically disqualifying him from participating in the favored pastime, he was a good golfer, giving him brownie points with Daddy. Daddy genuinely liked Reverend, keeping him in good favor. Such was not the case with Eskimo, Company CFO, who did not view Reverend with similar regard. From time to time, Reverend would pull some stunt that ended up costing The Company money. Being a bottom-line guy, Eskimo was not amused with these shenanigans and, therefore, had a perpetual hard-on for Reverend.

Eskimo, so named for his extreme fondness for the white powder named after a popular soft drink, had taken a unique route to his position as CFO. He was a bank teller in the institution where Daddy had his personal and company accounts. Daddy felt he provided good customer service and eventually hired Eskimo to work in the accounting department initially. Eskimo drank his way into Daddy's inner circle and was always front and center when Daddy held court. He was a Daddy wannabe, from copying his favorite expressions to matching him drink for drink. The nose candy allowed him to keep pace. In due course, when Daddy promoted him to CFO, Eskimo's reserved parking spot was adjacent to Daddy's with his initials on the accompanying sign. Eskimo was Livin' la Vida Loca.

Reverend, a fairly astute individual, sensed that Eskimo's patience with him was wearing extremely thin. So, he swung into action. Reverend was an accomplished guitar player who could read and write music. What better solution than to write a song in Daddy's honor? It was called "Where's Daddy?" and it went like this: "Took in a loan – was a real toughie – talked to John – he asked, Where's Daddy – Where's Daddy – Where's Daddy?"

It was nearing Christmas, and Daddy had again scheduled The Company Christmas party at Fair Lanes, the local Fairfax bowling alley. It was an annual drunk fest with loads of food and drink enjoyed by all. On the day of the party, Daddy customarily met with his inner circle at Artie's prior to heading to the bowling alley. They needed to develop a proper edge before wading into the festivities. After two hours of intense preparation, they were ready.

Upon entering Fair Lanes, Daddy headed directly to the front counter to rent bowling shoes. Reverend was behind the counter with a microphone and acoustic guitar in hand, flanked by ten Bugeaters. They dived right into a chorus of "Where's Daddy?" with Reverend taking the lead and the Bugeaters singing backup. It was a big hit. Daddy, with quite an edge on, was beaming. The dozens of non-Company people who had come to the bowling alley to roll a few strings were totally amused. They had never before and probably would never again witness anything like this display.

The party went on with its customarily drunken revelry. Daddy had collected fifty dollars apiece from each of the Bugeaters for the winner of a bowling contest. Instead of paying Reverend, who bowled the high score, Daddy took the five hundred dollars and handed it to Reverend's wife. He told her to "Get it the hell out of here before these clowns find a way to spend it." The raffle prize was announced as a dinner date with Bow, the Clown Prince. When Laura from post-closing pulled the winning ticket, Bow fell face down into his bowling lane. Surprisingly, she never made any effort to collect her prize.

Christmas and New Year's came and went. The Company was gearing up in preparation for a big Spring market. Eskimo had not forgotten Reverend's many transgressions. One Friday morning, after another Thursday night marathon at a local gin mill, Eskimo requested a meeting with Daddy. Ann, Daddy's secretary, ushered him in. Eskimo laid out a laundry list of instances where Reverend had screwed up, costing The Company money and embarrassment. He suggested they must take some action. Daddy stared at Eskimo. His eyes resembled two piss holes in a snowbank. He responded, "Can't fire the man. He wrote a song about me."

Because of Daddy's tolerance for most of the gravy train riders, it would have been easy to assume that he let everything go. That was not the case. On occasion, he exhibited a quick fuse in both firing and hiring people. There was the time he hired a so-called secondary marketing wizard. The wizard showed up and spent his initial two weeks sleeping at his desk. Then, Daddy summoned him to his office. He asked him to take a seat. He stared him down and then proclaimed, "I don't have any idea how this company is going to get along without you. But we're going to find out starting this afternoon."

Then there was The Company outing on the Dandy, a party boat that ran up and down the Potomac River. Launching from Alexandria, Virginia, the Dandy was an excellent venue for a booze cruise. Daddy leased it out for a Thursday night excursion. The troops showed up at 7:00 p.m. and proceeded to party into the wee hours of the morning. Pushing out the hundreds of drinks from behind the bar was a bombshell blonde with one helluva set of bodacious ta ta's. She did a great job of keeping the revelers tuned up. Daddy capped off the night by lavishing a very generous tip upon her.

Friday morning came way too soon, so only a few employees showed up for the opening bell. Mr. Z, having been unable to attend the party, was one of the few who made it on time. He was sitting in his office when Missy, the receptionist, rang him and said somebody was in the lobby to see Daddy. When Mr. Z came out, there stood the bombshell blonde.

"Can I help you?" asked Mr. Z.

"Yes. I am reporting for work."

"I see. And what position were you hired for?"

"I don't exactly know."

"You don't know?"

"Daddy told me to show up first thing this morning, so here I am."

"And what skill set do you bring?"

"I tend bar."

"Of course." Mr. Z had seen this movie before. "Missy. Would you ask Lisa D to come out, please?"

Lisa D, who managed the post-closing department, reported to the lobby.

"Lisa. This is – I'm sorry. I didn't get your name."

"Barbie."

"Boobie. I mean, Barbie here was asked by Daddy to report for work this morning. I'm sure she will fit right in with your group."

Lisa was not amused, but this also was not her first rodeo. Forcing a smile, she said, "Welcome aboard, Barbie. We will certainly put you to good use."

For all the boot-licking and ass-kissing continuously promulgated by the prominent train riders, no greater brown nosers existed than Big Marvin and his wife Karen, who worked in secondary marketing. They, of course, participated in the daily watering hole sessions, where they laughed at Daddy's jokes and storytelling and agreed with everything he said. They did his bidding and never questioned anything that he asked. But the naming of their firstborn son after Daddy put them way over the top. The fact that Daddy had two daughters and no sons made the naming even more significant. Aside from Daddy lavishing thousands of dollars of gifts upon the newborn, Big Marvin was named branch manager of the Woodbridge, Virginia office. Big Marvin and his wife had exceeded every train rider's expectations. Nobody even tried to outdo them.

Sometimes employees were forced to go beyond the call of duty to remain in good standing. Such was the case with Ann, Daddy's secretary, when he decided to bring his fishing talents to Texas. For all of the fishing they did compared to the drinking, they might as well have fished the pond outside of the Fairfax office. But Daddy enjoyed spinning tales of hunting and fishing in exotic outposts, the North Pole being one of them. Daddy brought the usual suspects down to Texas – Wall Street Joe, Mr. Z, Big Marvin, and Eskimo. They arrived in the evening and stayed up way too late drinking and playing cards.

They got up early the next morning and headed out to the lake, approximately thirty miles from the hotel out in the bush. After eight hard hours of drinking and fishing, they headed back toward the hotel in their rented van. They ran out of gas about halfway back on the one-lane country road.

Daddy's solution to the problem was to phone Ann at her desk in Fairfax. Daddy, who was totally lathered up, mumbled, "Got a bit of a problem. Van's out of gas." He then proceeded to pass out, just like the rest of the troops in the van.

Ann had more than a little bit of a problem. The only thing she knew was that these drunken yahoos were in Texas. Period. No city, no hotel, no nothing. Fortunately for Ann, she had been with Daddy for over ten years. Therefore, she had dealt with such adversity in the past, with her survival predicated on her ability to be highly resourceful. It did not help that there were five large lakes in the area, yet somehow, she uncovered where they were staying and, more amazingly, what lake they were fishing in. The hotel dispatched an employee with a full gas can in hand. He located the van and was amused to find the five occupants sound asleep. He gassed up the van and left a sign on the windshield which read, "You have gas."

Daddy and his boys eventually woke up and made it back to the hotel for another evening of drinking and card playing. In Daddy's world, déjà vu was a good thing. He would go to bed that night thanking his lucky stars that he paid Ann what he did. She was hands down worth her weight in gold.

Chapter 10

Realtors
(or Pigeons in the Park?)

Eddie the Pec made no secret about his less-than-shining opinion of realtors. As a group, the Bugeaters loved voting on and discussing the "Realtor of the Year Award" because of the many stories available and the nature of their interaction in realtors' daily activities.

The Bugeater membership featured some of the best BS-ers you might ever come across, but that number paled compared to their realtor counterparts. Just as Bow, the Clown Prince of Mortgage Banking, adhered to the principle that "an ignorant consumer is my best customer," so apparently did most members of the realtor community. Their marketing and advertising techniques were such that many must have seen the general public as nothing more than a bunch of buffoons.

For example, here are some common catch-phrases realtors use accompanied by their real meaning:

"Upgrades throughout" – A new doorknob was installed on the pantry door.

"Freshly painted and carpeted" – Three tenants ago.

"Great curb appeal" – The inside of the house is a disaster, but the grass was mowed.

"A motivated seller" – Property has been listed by five different agents and on the market for a year and a half.

Realtors (or Pigeons in the Park?)

"Priced to sell" – Listed at $100,000 over assessed value.

"A fixer-upper" – Must be torn down and completely rebuilt.

"Quiet cul-de-sac" – Backyard abuts the beltway.

"Great neighborhood" – Crime is down 10 percent this year.

"Your realtor for life" – Cannot be reached for post-closing issues once commission has been paid.

"Desirable school district" – Was considered top 10 in the county 30 years ago.

"Private hot tub" – Within view of only eight townhouse neighbors.

"Your dream home" – The realtor's only listing.

"Gorgeous inside" – Broken windows, needs roof replacement and an exterior paint job.

"Great amenities" – Any prospective buyers who inquired won't be called back.

"In-law suite" – Basement is piped up to install a bathroom.

"Worry-free living" – As long as one pays the $700-a-month condo fee.

"A well-qualified buyer" – Any buyer the realtor is working with, whether they are pre-approved or not.

"A motivated buyer" – Has already viewed 32 homes and whose time frame is within the next three years.

What could possibly motivate this difference between pitch and reality? The answer isn't very different than most real-life questions: follow the money. Or, in the case of realtors, follow the commission. Most people in this country work on a salary or an hourly scale. It is difficult for many to comprehend what it would be like to be compensated in any other way. However, the harsh reality of the real estate industry is that the realtor does not get paid unless the transaction they are working on goes to closing. Faced with getting paid versus the alternative, realtors will generally pull out all the stops – regardless of what that might entail. You might not condone their methods or approach, but on some level, we can all understand their will to survive.

Earl always theorized that this pay structure was at the root of the underlying nature of the real estate industry: It is and always will be a scapegoat business. The realtor typically functions at the hub of a transaction. Essentially, they put the transaction together and supposedly "manage" it. The realtor will refer to buyers the lender, the title company, the home inspection company, the termite company, and other necessary contact points, such as a contractor. Like most things, the more human beings you add to the mix, the chance of problems occurring increases dramatically – perhaps more so in the real estate industry. So, of course, when anything goes wrong, the first finger typically gets pointed at the realtor. Not being prone to accepting blame and accountability, the realtor will generally adopt a shotgun approach: fire away and hope most of the blame sticks elsewhere. Not to be outdone, lenders will blame realtors and title companies, and title companies will respond in kind – a perpetual vicious circle that has withstood the test of time. What is the common denominator? Nobody gets paid until and if the deal closes.

At one time or another, each of the Bugeaters had some interesting realtor experiences. Reverend was certainly no exception. When he first joined The Company, a realtor referred a loan to him for the first time. Reverend was pleased because it was difficult to cultivate new relationships. Also, if things went well, the realtor could be a consistent source of business. This particular loan was for a married couple. The husband was on assignment out of town when they contracted for the property sight unseen. Over time, this scenario consistently proves to be problematic. Things went well until closing time was approaching.

The borrowers ignored Reverend's requests to furnish the necessary documentation to complete the loan process. The realtor, of course, was badgering Reverend to wrap things up so she could bank the commission she had already spent.

At least twice daily, she asked him, "Are they approved? What is the problem? What are you doing about it?"

Finally, the husband informed Reverend that he had had the opportunity to view the house and was not pleased with it. "I'm not buying this house. She's trying to ram this sale down our throats, and I won't have it." Therefore, they were not going to supply the information. The loan would be rejected, and they would receive their earnest money deposit back.

Reverend had no recourse but to inform the realtor of this unfortunate change of circumstances.

The realtor became irate and informed Reverend in no uncertain terms, "You must force settlement."

"Huh?"

Reverend, new to the industry and The Company, was ignorant of the concept. So, he decided to seek the counsel of Tina, The Company's head closer.

Tina was a country girl from West Virginia who ran the closing department with an iron fist and maintained an excellent work ethic. She was an integral part of Daddy's well-oiled machine. And, like Daddy, she did not suffer fools easily.

Reverend interrupted her in the midst of another closing. He asked meekly, "Tina, how do I force a settlement?"

She scowled at first but then started laughing. "What the hell have you got yourself into this time? Understand this: If you don't get out of my face right now, I'm going to force my foot right up your ass. Be gone!"

Of course, Tina reported this event to the Bugeater leadership, leading Reverend to stockpile some additional points in his quest to become Mortgage Banker of the Year.

Reverend seemed to invite realtor confrontations. There was one realty office where he had spent a tremendous amount of time soliciting business with no results. Finally, a realtor felt sorry for him and threw Reverend a bone. His first loan out of that office! Forty-five days later, the loan closed on a Friday without incident. Reverend was on his way. He was going to knock 'em dead in that office going forward.

The following Monday, Reverend got dressed like he was going to his wedding and drove to the realty office first thing in the morning. He strutted in, basking in the glow of his Friday closing. He was working the crowd when a realtor beckoned him over to her desk.

She asked, "Are you Reverend?"

Reverend figured she must have heard of him and his good work. He replied, "Sure am. What can I do for you?"

She pulled one of his rate sheets off her desk, tore it into ten pieces, and threw it into the trash can.

"What you can do is never leave one of your goddamn rate sheets on my desk again. Take a hike!"

Reverend tried to shrug it off, figuring nothing ventured, nothing gained. Most of his rate sheets ended up in The Company dumpster anyway.

To add further insult to injury, prior to Christmas, the realty office manager informed Reverend that it would behoove him to provide the office with its holiday tree. Also, it had better be a Frazier Fir, the most expensive tree in Northern Virginia.

Reverend, who was used to constantly being shaken down by realtors, felt he had no choice. So, the next day, he drove forty miles in an ice storm, procured the desired tree, and delivered it to the office. As he stood soaking wet in the office lobby, realtor after realtor thanked him for the tree and promised substantial future business.

The manager proclaimed, "You ARE the man! You are our number one lender!"

Reverend now felt he had quite a future in this office. He returned two days later to cultivate these new relationships further. But the Frazier Fir was gone! He sought out the office manager and inquired, "What happened to my tree?"

She shook her head and said, "The building manager told us to take it out because it's a fire hazard. But it's all right. Sally Ann took it home."

Not only did Reverend have no idea who Sally Ann was, but the amount of future business he received from that office equaled John Belushi's cumulative grade point average in the *Animal House* movie – zero point zero.

Of course, Reverend was not the only Bugeater subject to realtor abuse. One day, when Earl started with The Company, he was out beating the streets trying to scare up some business in Falls Church. He dropped off some rate sheets in a realtor office when a realtor named Lynn H confronted him.

"Are you with The Company?" she asked.

Feeling some confidence, Earl responded, "Yes, I am."

She came back with, "Is Eddie still there?"

"Yup," said Earl.

Lynn H snarked, "As long as that piece of crap is still there, you will never get a loan out of this office. He screwed me over one too many times. Be gone!"

Earl put his tail between his legs and headed back out to The Company. He went straight to Eddie's office.

"Hey, Eddie," said Earl. "I ran into a friend of yours today."

"Who's that?"

"Lynn H."

"What?" said Eddie. "That piece of garbage? She's as useless as the tits on a boar. Did she trash me?"

Earl laughed. "Quite the contrary. She was most complimentary."

There was never such a formal proclamation in the universe of realtors, but there probably should have been: "Never let ethics stand in the way when trying to get a deal done." Perhaps this attitude could be applied to all types of businesses and industries, but it did appear to be particularly prevalent in real estate. Maybe it just seems that way with a large percentage of the population involved in at least one real estate transaction. Or perhaps it reverted to the underbelly of an industry where everybody is chasing the almighty dollar.

Consider the case of the realtor who listed the home of a military officer stationed overseas. The realtor had worked extremely hard to procure the listing and had, in essence, promised the gentleman the moon. The realtor had convinced her client that to put the home in selling shape, the work would cost $5,000 and take approximately 30 days. She told him her contractor guaranteed a great price for the work and would do an excellent job.

"This work is what you need to get your house sold," she declared to the military officer. "I'll take care of everything for you. I just need the funds."

The officer agreed and forwarded a bank check for the $5,000. The realtor immediately contacted several female and male colleagues to announce the listing and to describe the oversized private hot tub sitting in the backyard.

"Here we go again, guys," she crowed. "Wait till you see this place."

She took a portion of the funds and bought a significant amount of liquor and food while setting up the first of many hot tub parties over the following month. It was difficult to determine whether more sex occurred in the tub or the house, but the bottom line was that there was plenty of it. Perhaps the listing realtor could rationalize what went on since all of the invitees were realtors.

Was she an unscrupulous rogue or a marketing genius? At the end of the month, she had "her contractor" mickey up an invoice for $5,000 for the work that was never done. The house never sold, but that did not preclude her from sending the owner refrigerator magnets and postcards periodically asking for referrals. Humility was not her strong suit.

In another instance, Reverend was once again on the wrong end of a realtor's gun. He had been soliciting this realtor for several months but had gotten nowhere. The realtor was a top producer at what many thought was the leading realty firm in the country. His name and picture adorned listing signs all over Northern Virginia. In short, everyone considered him to be a big swinging dick. Reverend waltzed into this realtor's office one afternoon, and the big hitter motioned him over to his desk. After making small talk, the realtor invited Reverend to his home for dinner that Saturday night. Reverend was ecstatic! This could be the meal ticket he had been longing for. When he told his wife about it, she couldn't have been happier.

Saturday night rolled around, and Reverend showed up at the realtor's house on time. The home was enormous and very well decorated. The meal in the oven smelled divine, which was great because Reverend was famished. The realtor asked Reverend to take a seat at the kitchen table because he had something he wanted him to look at. The realtor reappeared two minutes later and laid down the most recent federal tax return for one of his clients.

"Take a look at this and see what you think," the realtor said.

Reverend was not known for his ability to analyze tax returns, but he thought he would be wise to wing it. After a cursory review, he asked the realtor what size home he was attempting to locate for the buyer.

"McLean, Great Falls; something around a mil will do," noted the realtor.

Reverend almost choked. Even he knew the buyer couldn't come close to qualifying for that price range. "I have to be honest with you," Reverend stammered. "I don't think he can get approved for that much money."

"I know that," snorted the realtor. "You need to make it work."

Reverend had a puzzled look on his face.

"Juice up the numbers," said the realtor. "My client is counting on me, and I'm counting on you."

"You mean, falsify the return? I can't do that!" cried Reverend.

The realtor stood up and offered his hand to Reverend.

"Lenders that work for me make it happen," he said. "I can see you don't really want to be successful. Have a nice evening."

Ten minutes later, Reverend was wolfing down a Big Mac with fries at the local McDonalds.

Like his Bugeater colleagues, Earl had his share of realtor stories. However, as opposed to Eddie, Earl relied almost exclusively upon realtors for purchase and refinance referrals. He was most fortunate to develop relationships with several realtors that he ended up working with for more than twenty years. They were good, hard-working realtors and good people to boot. Many were ex-military folks. Some were West Point graduates. They had large and loyal client bases due to their work ethic and determination to provide excellent service. They understood the industry was fraught with problems and that choosing a rational approach rather than a confrontational one worked best. Earl's wife had worked as a realtor when their children were young. They both considered themselves blessed and thankful for Earl's referral base, especially given the bevy of extracurricular activity swirling around the Northern Virginia real estate scene.

The fact that realtors typically functioned as the hub of real estate transactions placed them in an advantageous position. And they were well aware of it. If you happened to be one of the spokes in the wheel attached to the hub, there was a price to pay. Lenders, title companies, and home inspectors were constantly forced or shamed into ponying up.

Remuneration came in many different shapes and forms. For example, realtors would hold brokers opens on Tuesdays to showcase homes they had listed for sale. They would provide and advertise an expensive lunch to attract as many realtors as possible. They would, of course, lean on lenders to foot the bill, promising they would get the loan when the house sold.

There were two fallacies associated with this process. One, the realtors would only show up to get the free lunch after calling around to see who was serving what. And two, the lenders never got the loan because the realtor bringing the buyers to the property usually controlled that, not the listing agent.

As Reverend was well aware, realtors loved to cash in on the festive holiday season. They would throw lavish Christmas parties for their clients and potential clients. The holiday revelers rarely knew that the beholding lenders and title companies furnished the food and drink.

One of Reverend's colleagues suffered the ultimate indignity at his own Christmas party. Eric held a Christmas happy hour with food at a local expensive restaurant. Reverend showed up at 6:00 p.m. when the party was in full swing. He sauntered up to two realtors who were stuffing their faces like there was no tomorrow. He waited for one to wipe the barbeque sauce off her face and then introduced himself.

Realtors (or Pigeons in the Park?)

After making small talk about the industry, he asked, "So, ladies, how long have you been referring loans to Eric?"

The barbeque sauce lady looked puzzled and asked, "Who's Eric?" She then turned to her colleague and said, "We'd best be going now. I heard that other lender is serving shrimp at his party."

Given all the ways that crafty realtors came up with to extract favors from their industry "partners," Eddie was party to perhaps the most shameless request possible. Through the years, realtors came up with the concept of charging purchasers an "administration fee," usually $395, to be paid with the closing costs at settlement. This fee was in addition to their commission, which the sellers typically paid. Over time, purchasers questioned the necessity of paying this fee and began to balk at it.

Eddie was courting a new realtor for business when the gentleman offered to buy him lunch. Eddie's antenna went up immediately – it was the first time a realtor had offered to buy.

They met at an expensive eatery, and the realtor got right to the point. He noted that more and more buyers were refusing to pay the admin fee, but his broker was adamant that it be collected.

"I am embarrassed to ask my people to pay this fee," exclaimed the realtor. "It's just putting more money in the broker's pocket."

The realtor, whose commission on a transaction was more than triple that of a loan officer, suggested that Eddie would get all of his future business and that of his office colleagues if he paid the purchasers' admin fees.

Eddie almost choked on his salad. "Let me get this straight. You want ME to pay a fee that your broker is trying to jam on your customers?"

Eddie thought he had heard it all, but the gall of this realtor's proposal floored him. He politely said that he would take it under consideration and get back to the realtor very soon.

What he really wanted to say was, "Don't hold your breath."

Chapter 11

Loan Applicants or Victims?

Every business known to mankind has customers. Every business has a product to sell to its customers. The mortgage banking industry is no different. Its customers are the many folks who aspire to achieve the American Dream of home ownership but cannot afford to pay cash. Even the few with the wherewithal to pay cash many times take out a mortgage due to the favorable income tax provisions available for writing off mortgage interest and real estate taxes. Over decades, the vast majority of Americans have taken out a mortgage to buy or refinance their homes and thus have experienced the mortgage process. The process has changed dramatically over this time frame as the industry evolved due to innovation, technology, and regulatory oversight.

Eddie the Pec, de facto figurehead of the Bugeater Lunch and Supper Club, experienced these pronounced changes firsthand. One of eight children, he grew up in rural Nebraska. When he was ten, his parents decided to buy a house in town. They always liked the looks of the home, and the location was good. His dad announced his intentions to the existing owner. They drew up a one-page document that served as a real estate contract. He said he would get down to the local bank as soon as possible.

When Eddie's dad said he was heading to the bank to take care of the house loan two days later, young Eddie asked if he could tag along. His dad agreed, stating that he might learn something. Little did Eddie know that this visit would be the first of hundreds of mortgage transactions that he would be involved in or witness. It is probably safe to say that many of his future applicants would rue the day he was exposed to the mortgage business.

Loan Applicants or Victims?

Father and son walked into the bank and all of the tellers greeted them by name. The bank president ushered them into his office. He was extremely happy to see them. They exchanged pleasantries and got caught up on their respective families' happenings.

"So, Ed, what brings you and young Eddie down here today?" asked the bank official.

"We've decided to buy the Jones' place," Ed stated.

"Nice place. Plenty of room for your brood. You know the barn needs some work?"

"Yeah, Bobbie said he can knock it off pretty soon."

"Good. He took care of my fence last week. How much ya need?"

"Ten K."

"Okay. Stop and see Margaret this afternoon. She'll have your check for you."

"Thanks. Come by and have supper when you get the chance."

"Will do."

The mortgage banking industry was born in the late 1970s when a Wall Street wizard developed the concept of securitizing mortgages in bundles. In essence, a security was created that could be traded just like any other Wall Street instrument. Hence, a cottage industry came into existence, with mortgage-backed securities traded routinely, leading to the development of mortgage banking firms operating in contrast to the typical hometown bank. Whereas the bank created a mortgage and collected the interest on it until the homeowner paid it off, the typical mortgage bank operated in a manner that befitted the fast-buck industry it came to personify. "Get it in, get it out, and get paid" was the modus operandi.

It was relatively easy to set up a mortgage banking operation. The principals needed a certain amount of net worth and little else. Some firms aligned themselves with banks that functioned to fund the mortgage loans at the settlement table and then sold the loans to large banks that would service them. Those companies without bank affiliation would set up warehouse lines with banks used to fund the loans. Post settlement, they would sell the loans to large banks for lucrative fees, pay off the warehouse line, and then move on to the next one. It was a rock and roll business that, in a good real estate market, could quickly generate billions of dollars.

Beyond the aforementioned required financial setup, one needed office space, equipment, and manpower. Manpower consisted of salaried employees such as underwriters, processors, closers, post closers, and shippers. And then, of course, those who would bring the business in the door. Loan originators. Typically, one hundred percent commissioned salesmen. Licenses, education, or credentials not required. All anyone needed was a desire to throw their hat into the ring of the fastest-growing fast-buck industry in the country. The meek need not apply. Hence, the diverse and fascinating background of the Bugeater membership.

As previously noted, the Washington Post wrote a scathing article condemning the unscrupulous practices of loan originators (see end of chapter). After recovering from the initial shockwaves generated within the local mortgage banking and real estate community, the Bugeaters actually embraced the article, because the author referred to loan applicants as "victims." The Bugeaters loved it. Henceforth, the daily conversation ran as such. "Hey, Bow. How many victims do you have coming in today?" "One more than you got, Eddie. Gonna ring the cash register. Cha-ching, you yo-yo."

Loan Applicants or Victims?

It is important to note that cultivating relationships with victims was paramount to the success of many members in winning some of the annual awards. And those who rose to the pinnacle and were voted Mortgage Banker of the Year all exhibited some degree of ability and willingness to fleece their customers. Some, like Bow, the Clown Prince, were absolute masters of their craft. This talent, of course, kept him in the good graces of Johnny Gumba, who was all about the bottom line. Others just stumbled into it. The net result was everybody was making money hand over fist.

Earl was at the office one morning, sitting at his desk, trying to organize his day, when Reverend wandered in. As they were making small talk, Reverend's phone rang. Earl was not paying attention to the phone conversation until he heard, "Mrs. Chen, I really wish it could be one. Have a nice day."

Earl was flabbergasted. He said, "Tell me I didn't hear what I just heard."

Reverend, red-faced and a bit sheepish, admitted that Mrs. Chen did, in fact, get jacked up. As always, the story was convoluted but played out something like this. Mrs. Chen was referred to Reverend for a refinance of her home by one of the realtors he did business with. Everything went fairly smoothly until the loan hit underwriting. Mrs. Chen's income was not quite what Reverend had calculated it to be (or rather, guessed at), and the underwriter was having trouble approving the loan. As in all such situations, the file ended up on Johnny Gumba's desk. Gumba summoned Reverend to his office.

"Where the hell did you come up with this income?" asked an exasperated Gumba.

"It's what we need to qualify," spurted out the embarrassed Reverend.

"Lovely," said Johnny. "Well, you're lucky I'm going to straighten this out for you. Now, get your ass on the telephone and tell old Mrs. Chen she doesn't qualify for a Fannie Mae loan but we can go with a Freddie Mac. Now, what do you have in this thing?"

"One point," said Reverend.

"Well, it just became two. Now handle it."

Reverend was not one to embrace confrontation. Hence, his concept of handling the situation was to ignore it. Mrs. Chen arrived at the settlement table and, upon review of the HUD 1 settlement sheet, discovered it cost her two points, inflating the cost by $3,000. She phoned Reverend and said, "You tell me loan cost one point. I come to closing and there are two points."

Reverend's response is duly noted and became legendary among the Bugeater membership. Of further note was that Freddie Mac loans cost the same as Fannie Mae. Johnny Gumba had perfected the practice of allegedly "switching" the loan to Freddie Mac to make it work and thus charging whatever the situation would bear. It became fondly known as "the Freddie Mac Special."

The "Special" fit well into the Clown Prince's bag of tricks. He had, of course, mastered using the aforementioned fictional "Committee" that helped line his pockets. Bow would size up the victim and surrounding circumstances and then make a determination as to whether they could be fleeced, and if so, what method would be appropriate. (See The Article at the end of Chapter 6.)

One day, the Bugeaters were coming back from another lunch at L&N Seafood, when Missie the receptionist informed Bow that a gentleman named Brent was on the phone. Bow's face turned the color of a new fire engine. The Bugeaters were delighted; they

Loan Applicants or Victims?

knew, once again, he was on the ropes with an irate customer. Earl, Eddie, and Mr. Miller followed Bow back to his office to enjoy his discomfort and listen to the song and dance he put out there. An established Bugeater practice was to gather in the colleague's office when they were in trouble to revel in their misery. Bow told Brent he was in the middle of something and would call him back.

Turns out, Brent was calling from the settlement table. After the settlement sheet was reviewed by all parties present, it was determined Brent was being asked to swallow an extra $3,500 in points. The Clown Prince had gotten lazy on this one. He forgot to convey one of his BS reasons for the inflated cost. However, he was having a slow month, so he needed the extra profit. Unbeknownst to Bow, they were also scrutinizing his Good Faith Estimate (GFE) sheet at the table. Of course, he had not disclosed the extra point he instructed the closer to throw into the closing pot.

Had Bow sized up the situation properly, he would have realized that Brent would not go away easily. As all parties to the transaction sat and seethed, Bow did not bother to call Brent back, increasing the tension for all. So, they decided to spring into action. The realtor who referred the loan to Bow called and proceeded to put the listing agent, real estate broker, settlement agent, and seller on the line. Bow bobbed and weaved like an experienced prize fighter. After these individuals threw their hands up in frustration, Brent grabbed the phone. He went into an expletive-laced tirade that lasted two minutes. Upon completion, Bow responded, "Brent, I'm really glad you got your house. Take care." The Bugeaters were beside themselves. To the Clown Prince, it was like water rolling off a duck's back.

Those familiar with the business world and customer service, in general, might wonder if these victims took these many affronts lying down. Whatever happened to "Let me speak to your manager" and "The customer is always right"? Rest assured; The Company was no different. Johnny Gumba had a very disciplined approach to these situations. First, he made sure every call from a disgruntled customer came to him, not Daddy. Although Daddy was also a bottom-line guy, his tolerance level for such shenanigans came up well short of Gumba's. He did not suffer embarrassment well at all. Johnny did not know how to spell embarrassment. The almighty buck was the quid pro quo for having to constantly deal with these malcontents. As long as he or the loan officer could juice up the profit on a transaction, nothing they could say had any effect. His lavish lifestyle and many vices took precedence.

A tactic well known to the Bugeaters and fairly prevalent throughout the mortgage banking industry was to furnish a low-ball Good-Faith Estimate to loan applicants (or victims). There was really no law or regulation that governed how they completed the GFEs. In those days, the industry was basically left to police itself. Similar to the proverbial fox guarding the hen house. A savvy loan originator knew that when a potential customer demanded a GFE before deciding on who to do the mortgage with, they were dealing with a rate shopper of the highest degree. Therefore, they would furnish a Good Faith Estimate that appeared favorable compared to others submitted correctly (or in genuine good faith). To save closing cost money, the victim would often choose the low-ball offer. These originators (see the Clown Prince) had a plethora of excuses and BS explanations as to why there was a difference between an estimate and actual closing costs. As long as the loan closed and they got paid, all was well in their world, where a good reputation didn't buy one a new suit or pay the rent.

Eddie was known to, on occasion, lighten up on an estimate in the interest of procuring more business. He would not, of course, admit to such an exception and seemed able to dance around the issue. For example, he was refinancing an elderly couple for the third time. These were not your run-of-the-mill clients. They owned a million-dollar townhome in Georgetown. The husband had retired from a high-level position in the Nixon administration, and the wife, an attorney, had reported directly to Bowie Kuhn, the Commissioner of Major League Baseball. Eddie and the settlement agent were going to the couple's home to conduct the closing. Just as they were leaving the office to proceed to the closing, they discovered the couple had eight months of real estate taxes to pay before they could consummate the settlement. In other words, they had to write a check for $9,000 US when they had expected to break even. Eddie was heavily sweating when he asked the settlement agent to call ahead and drop the bomb on the couple. The agent agreed to do so since he got a lot of business from Eddie and hoped to continue the relationship.

They arrived at the couple's home on time, and the husband ushered them into the living room. The wife, who had dealt with Eddie in the past, looked up and said, "Good afternoon, gentlemen. Let's get this circle jerk started."

The couple, after much consternation, signed the closing papers. They were not pleased but did not want to cut off their nose to spite their face. The numbers made sense, so they bit the bullet. Once again, Eddie rang the cash register.

After getting back to the office, Eddie ran into Earl in the lobby.

"How did that big closing go, Eddie?" asked Earl.

With a big smile, Eddie replied, "Another satisfied customer!"

Eddie was generally good at controlling a situation, but on occasion, met his match. There was the time he was referred to a car salesman at one of the local big car dealerships. Eddie was trying to line up the loan application but was having difficulty as the pair continued to play phone tag. Finally, they connected.

"Pleased to meet you, sir," said Eddie. "I'm glad we are able to talk. Do you know what time and day you can come by my office for your loan application?"

"I will need you to come by the dealership," said the salesman. "I am a very busy man."

Eddie did not want to drive to Tysons Corner, especially during rush hour. "It would be best if you could come to my office," said Eddie. "Just in case we need some info that would be at hand."

"Listen, Eddie," barked the salesman. "I don't believe you are reading this situation correctly. Number one, I am the customer. Number two, I am giving you business. And number three, and most importantly, I am the straw that stirs the drink."

Eddie determined that maybe driving to Tysons Corner wasn't so bad after all.

Chapter 12

The Journey

When a person is going to buy a house, what do they do? How do they start out? And how do they end up? The journey is all the crazy stuff that goes on in between. One of the things that prompted Earl to put this book together was that many people didn't understand the process or why and how different things happened. There was always an element of mystery to the whole thing, so he thought it would be good to outline it from A to Z with examples. Then people may read it and say, "Oh, geez, yeah, that happened to me. And now I know what they're talking about."

How does it all start out? For example, parents living in a townhouse with two kids and a third on the way say to each other, "We need to get a bigger place. So, what do we do now?" The first step is interviewing realtors to sell their existing home and put them into a new home. A quick definition here: The listing agent sells the existing home, and the buyer's agent finds the new home. For the most part, the same person does both roles. If you like them, why would you change? Although it happens sometimes. So, when it comes to what will happen first, the focus is selling the existing home because you typically must sell before you can buy the next one.

Realtors tend to embellish things, and they are salesmen by trade. For example, when being interviewed by prospective sellers they would inflate the price of the house. In other words, if the house is worth 500k, they come in and say, "Oh, I can get you 540k," knowing full well that they can't. And then, if they interview an honest realtor who says, "Oh, I can get you $500k," the people say, "Well, wait a minute, we're leaving 40 grand on the table here, so we're going to go with the first realtor we interviewed." Therefore, the chosen realtor's strategy is to list the house at $540k, even though the comparable sales support $500k. Typically, the house would sit on the market for two weeks, with nobody submitting any offers. Then the realtor would advise the sellers, "We're going to have to lower this price to $500k," which is where the honest realtor had proposed setting the price. Unfortunately, that's how it's often done.

It's not the intent to portray all realtors in this way. Like anything, there's the good, the bad, and the mediocre. For example, a realtor will convince people that to sell their house, they must do X—paint the walls neutral, re-carpet, put some extra shrubs in by the front entrance, whatever it is—which leads us to the next story.

Earl was selling the house he and his wife were living in, and he was going to build a new one. A good friend of his was a realtor, Frank. Frank called Earl the day after they put the house on the market and said, "Hey, I want to come by and see the house." So, Earl said, "Oh, great. Yeah, come on by tomorrow." He thought Frank was bringing a client by because he used to refer his buyers to Earl for loans all the time; they did a lot of business together. So, the next day, Frank comes by with his wife. The two couples knew each other because they also socialized together. The only thing was, no buyer was with them. Earl was puzzled and said, "What are you guys doing? Where's the customer?" Frank laughs and says, "Oh, no, no, we want to buy the house." "Oh! Wow!" For Earl, it was the easiest negotiation. "Well, what do you want to pay for it?" "We'll pay what you listed." All right. That was the end of that.

This story illustrates how a realtor can sometimes steer a seller in the wrong direction. Earl's mother-in-law, who was very artistic, had painted many of the rooms in the house and added a border strip of wallpaper along the top of the walls. While preparing their home for sale, Earl and his wife went with the theory of neutralizing it by repainting the walls and removing the wallpaper borders. Then, when Frank and his wife came back, they exclaimed, "Oh, why did you do that? We loved that stuff!"

The number one way a realtor shows the seller that they're doing something to sell the house is by arranging an open house. The open house is a strategic concept; they rarely sell houses. So why do realtors put them on? It's not to sell the house, and they know full well that hosting an open house will probably not sell it. What they're actually trying to do is pick up prospective buyers who they can represent, who come by, take a look, and say, "Well, I don't want to buy this one" so the realtor says, "Okay, but I can help you find another one." So, that is often the motive behind the open house.

Realtors also put on what they call a "broker's open," which is exclusively for other realtors and traditionally done on a Tuesday at lunchtime. These realtors would shake down a title company or a lender to provide the catering for it. So, most of the realtors attending are looking for a free lunch. They would call around and ask, "What are you serving?" One guy had shrimp, oh, but this guy's got lobster. That's the way it was. Again, the realtor was trying to show the seller they're doing something, but the broker's open doesn't typically sell the home.

Okay, the house is listed. Potential buyers have come by and seen it. Maybe the open house works! And now some offers are coming in. The way the industry works, the buyer's realtor could not submit their offer to the seller's realtor without what they call prequalification letters or preapproval letters from lenders. Meaning that the buyer had gone to a lender and submitted an application. And the lender says, "Oh, you're qualified for this much money." And so when the realtors would submit their buyer's contract offer to the seller's realtor, they would always include a prequal or preapproval letter. Companies typically had standard approval letters because there were legalities involved, and most of these letters had more disclaimers than a hospital admittance form.

For example, you might get this loan if the sun's out, the wind is blowing no more than five mph, and the sky is blue. It was kind of an industry joke, like, what does this really mean? Again, there's a lot of stuff that must happen behind the scenes, and the lenders who were doing their proper job had the people come in and bring their pay stubs and bank statements, and they would pull a credit report. By doing a thorough job, the letter was solid in the absence of something flying out of the woodwork that nobody knew about. Then there were loan officers who bluffed, and the Bugeaters had plenty of them. Like, "Yeah, it looks good, whatever." They would just write the letter and send it to the realtor. For example, Bow, the Clown Prince, would be home drunk on a Tuesday night and some realtor would call him at 10 o'clock and say, "Hey, can you qualify this guy?" And Bow, without talking to the potential buyer, would say, "Okay. Here's your letter," and he's thinking, "I hope this is going to work."

According to their nature, the realtors would sometimes be antagonistic, and often, they would question the letters, probably with good reason. One time, Earl had a situation with this particular realtor, Bill—they did a lot of business together. There was a listing agent in the area who sold a lot of homes there. He could be a pain in the ass. Bill would call Earl up, and say, "Hey, Earl. Our buyer is going to write an offer on that house, and we need the approval letter." He'd think, "Damn, it's that listing agent again." So, Earl would submit the letter. Then, Bill calls him back, saying, "The listing agent wants you to change this and that and the other thing." And Earl said, "All right." So, he changes the letter and sends it in again. The listing agent comes back, wanting Earl to change this and that, and now Earl's getting really ticked off. He makes the changes and sends in the letter. Then, the listing agent comes back a third time. So, Earl says, "Bill, let me deal with it." Earl picks up the phone, calls the listing agent, and says, "Hey, why don't we do this? Why don't you write the letter? And if I like it, I'll sign it." The listing agent finally capitulated and accepted the letter. That was the kind of thing the Bugeaters could run into.

Many loan officers would just issue the letters without even reviewing the borrower's paperwork, throw it at the wall, and hope that it sticks; modus operandi. When a customer did not qualify for the loan, the loan officer would blame various things such as the interest rates went up. When the customer applied, the rate was five percent, and now it's seven, and they can't qualify at the higher rate (even if the rates were falling, they gave this excuse). In these cases, everybody involved in the transaction is freaking out because the people really want the house, and the realtor is counting on getting that commission, and now maybe they won't. The lender is on the hot seat; everybody is calling them. So, as a last-ditch option, they could refer the loan to a subprime lender who charges exorbitant rates, but almost anybody can get a loan. However, it was an oxymoron that the borrower can't qualify at seven, yet the subprime lender can qualify them at eight. The subprime lender charges a high premium on the rate to offset the risk of the customer defaulting on the loan. So, they were taking the risk that it would work out. They can make so much more money that way. And then, of course, the loan officer who screwed up in the first place, who should have been able to qualify the loan and didn't, ends up getting a referral fee from the subprime lender. So now everybody's happy, right?

So, now they're in the stage where the realtor who listed the house is entertaining the offers. There are several things to evaluate, such as the submitted letters. If there are two companies, two potential buyers working with two lenders, and everything else is pretty much the same, and if the realtor knew the reputation of those lenders – one is good, and one is bad – they would go with the good one.

But there was another interesting element. In addition to the approval letters, when the realtors evaluated these contracts, they also looked at the type of loans used. There are three types of loans: conventional, VA, and FHA.

FHA is Federal Housing Administration (government loans insured by HUD), and VA is the Veterans Administration (government loans with their own program for the veterans) – HUD is Housing and Urban Development. Conventional loans are sold to Fannie Mae and Freddie Mac – nicknames for Federal National Mortgage Association and Federal Home Loan Mortgage Corporation.

The problem with the government loans was that traditionally, the property appraisals for those loans had more stringent requirements. So, when a listing realtor was looking at that, they would take the conventional loan because they didn't want the appraiser to potentially come in with a lower value or require repairs because of the more stringent requirements. So, unfortunately, it worked against the FHA buyers, many of whom were first-time buyers, and VA buyers, the veterans, especially in a rising market, where sometimes the FHA and VA appraisals didn't support the higher prices. However, the conventional appraisers had more liberal guidelines to arrive at their higher valuations.

Let's go back a step to when the buyers select the lender who would write that approval letter for them. Some buyers would listen to the realtor and work with their recommended lender, while others wanted to shop for ten different lenders. The realtor is the manager of the entire process – they refer the lender, the title company, the termite company, and the home inspector – everything reflects upon the realtor. If the whole transaction from contract to settlement went well, then, of course, they would get more referral business.

When the buyers choose their lender, if they were rate shoppers and all they cared about was saving a couple of bucks, that played right into the hands of a guy like Bow the Clown Prince because he allegedly had the best quotes in town. So, if they called him up when everybody else was at 6% and he was at 5.75%, they would think, "Oh, wow, this is great." However, since the interest rate could not be locked until there was a house address to lock it into, there was always a gap in time between when the rate was quoted and when it could be locked in. It could be a week later; it could be two weeks later. So then, magically, when the people contract for the house, suddenly, the Clown Prince's rates are just like everybody else's. The buyer would question that, and Bow would say, "Oh, well, rates are going up, and this and that and the other thing," but that was his modus operandi.

Once the sale contract is fully ratified and a settlement date is set, generally, the first thing that happens next is a home inspection, which can cause a lot of problems, too. Many times, the buyers will see a piece of dust in the corner and say, "Oh, fix that," and then it's back and forth with "I'm not going to fix this" and "You've got to fix this." Generally, they'll come to some agreement. Interestingly enough, in certain markets when the inventory is low, and you have ten different contract offers on a house, many buyers will come in with an offer and waive the home inspection clause because it's so competitive. Then the next guy who comes in with the home inspection clause will lose out because the seller says, "Hell no, no home inspection, I'm not going to worry about fixing anything." And that becomes buyer beware because there could be some serious problems, like a cracked foundation or a bad roof. So, let's say that a home inspection gets done and passed. So now, they officially apply for the mortgage. That's when the buyers must assemble a bunch of information, like pay stubs and bank statements, and the lender would have done a credit report initially, just on the qualifying piece. There's a lot of documentation involved. The loan officers, who were doing a good job, assembled all this stuff, put it into a package, and gave it to the processor. And that was the way it was supposed to be done. But of course, then somebody like the Clown Prince would leave it up to his processor, who at times was Charli, and she'd have to chase the borrowers down and tell them what they needed to do and what documentation to provide – Bow never explained any of that to them. And again, that was all part of the good, the bad, and the mediocre.

Earl typically set up face-to-face appointments with his borrowers in those days. The business has changed a lot now, where everyone does

The Journey

everything online, and the loan originators often don't even meet the customers. But in those days, the good loan officers wanted to meet the customers because they could sit down with them, explain everything, answer any questions, and give details to them. And they could lay out the journey: A, B, C, D, so they understood it, no surprises, and then it would typically go smoothly because they all knew everybody had their marching orders and knew what they had to do.

Of course, there were different approaches. For example, one time Bow the Clown Prince had three loan applications going on at the same time. So, he'd be in one office, tick off those customers, then go to the next office and tick off the next ones, and then rotate to the third; he just kept going in a circle. By the time he was done, it was a mess.

At 11 o'clock one day, Bow came in to meet his customer. He looked nervous, so Earl went out to the hallway to make small talk with him. Earl said, "Bow, what's the matter? You look a little upset here." Bow says, "Oh, this guy was in here yesterday, and he's coming back today. I sold him a 7-23 loan. And he wants me to explain it to him." And Earl said, "Well, what's wrong with that?" And Bow replies, "Because I don't have any idea how that damn thing works, you know?" So, the borrower comes in. As the Bugeaters typically did, they went down the hall to stand outside Bow's office. Bow had his elbow on the desk about a foot from the other guy who had his elbow on the desk, and they were just staring at each other. And it was just comical, but it was an example of how these loan applications can go.

One day, Earl was in an application with a woman who had come in with two young children. Earl had his head down, scratching up the paper application while she was giving him information. In the middle of it, Earl looked up to see that her four-year-old had drawn a snowman on his wall with a black crayon. So, Earl looked at the woman and said, "I see you have a budding artist here." And she said, "Excuse me?" Earl said, "Take a look." After she turned around and saw the artwork on the wall, she was concerned, and Earl just said, "Don't worry about it." Those paint cans under his desk make more sense now, right?

Another time, a couple came in with a young kid, and everything was coming at Earl at once, and he could hardly keep up with it. He was filling in the application while his pager was going off, his landline was ringing, call after call after call, and he was trying to get the information from the couple. Their son, who was three or four years old, was underneath Earl's desk, pulling on his pant legs. Earl tried to shake him off—to no avail. Trying to be polite, he made it through and never forgot that one.

Earl tells the story of a series of car commercials back in the day, set in a car dealership, that are still the funniest commercials he's ever seen. The first commercial shows a couple sitting at the desk, ready to buy a car. The car salesman, bearing a strong resemblance to a Gestapo officer, is dressed up in a big trench coat and holding a cigarette holder. He's standing in front of the desk looking at the couple with this paperwork in front of them. They can't figure out what's what. Then the car salesman says "Sign za papers, sign za papers." The wife is all nervous and says to her husband, "Stan, what should we do? Should we sign the papers?" Stan is all frazzled, so they just walk out! Then, in the next commercial, Stan and his wife come back the next day. When they come in, Stan is ready to put his foot down. He bangs his fist on the desk and he says, "I want to know what my payment is going to be." The salesman sitting at the desk says, "Oh, you want to know what your payment's gonna be? Sure." So, he turns around, and a big curtain opens to show a nice-looking young lady standing there, and she's got a wheel. She spins the wheel, and it lands on $439 a month, so the salesman says, "That'll be $439 a month. Congratulations!" Then he puts a cigar in his mouth. These commercials served as an inspiration to the Bugeaters.

In the Bugeater chapter, it was noted that the Bugeater Lunch and Supper Club was formulated in the summer of 1988, in the era of digital pagers, where they only got the phone number of who was calling. That evolved into the voice pagers. It was during that time when they broke into the voice pager of Bow the Clown Prince and changed his message to mess with him. The old digital pagers served their purpose. But the typical thing would be for Earl to be driving, out trying to make sales calls, and it'd be pouring rain, and his pager would go off. He'd see it was from Mount Vernon Realty, for example. Great, somebody's calling for a deal, right? So, Earl would pull over on the side of the road where there was a phone booth. He'd go into the booth where the roof was leaking and call into Mount Vernon Realty.

"Hello, Mount Vernon Realty."

"Hey, this is Earl returning the page."

"Yeah, hang on." A minute later. "No, nobody called you."

"Oh, thanks a lot."

Then, a minute later, buzz buzz, there's another page with the Mount Vernon Realty number. Next phone booth, he'd get soaked again.

"No, nobody here called you, sorry."

And then the next day, the realtor would call Earl and say, "You never called me back yesterday."

Earl's like, "Yeah, okay."

Some of those Realty companies had sixty agents, and the one who paged him was probably out for coffee.

The pagers evolved from the digital to the voice pagers, and then eventually when the cell phones came in, the Bugeaters got them, but they started out with the digital pagers.

Real estate closings typically take thirty days. One would turn a file in, and the processor would order the appraisal, and the appraisals took a while to get back. And then the processor had to start verifying stuff. Eventually, they would put together everything they thought they needed. Then, they would submit it to underwriting, and underwriting would look at it and inevitably come up with something else they wanted. So, then they'd have to go back and contact the customers who would say, "Why do you need this? And why didn't you tell me about that before?" And the processor would say, "We didn't know about it because the underwriter just came up with it," and then it would go back and forth and sideways. That was a normal process. Then they would get it approved, the closing date set, and the closing papers sent over to the title company. The title company could then combine it with their paperwork and create a closing package. And then the people would come in on Tuesday morning at 10 and sign the papers, and now they own the house. That was the normal process.

Now, many times, Bow would submit a loan three days prior to the closing date. And many would ask, "Why would he do that?" The answer was always, "Well, just because he is Bow." He sat on it and was busy with golf courses and bowling alleys. So, he would turn in the file, the processor would go berserk because now they've got a 30-day process that's going to get condensed into three days, which means scramble, scramble, scramble. And then Bow would go down to Daddy's office with some half-assed reason as to why he just submitted the loan that had to settle in three days. And it was always his "best agent" that he was dealing with every single time (even though they were all different agents), so the staff would have to scramble. And it would get done because Daddy knew that was how his bread was buttered, getting these loans closed. It was all about the referral business. Therefore, it always got done. And then, of course, Bow would prance around in the real estate office and tell everybody what a great job he had done. Meanwhile, he didn't do a damn thing.

When it comes to underwriters, like everything else, there were good underwriters, bad underwriters, and mediocre underwriters. And the bad ones were bad. Many times, if an underwriter approved a loan, and somehow it went into default, Daddy or anybody who was CEO of a mortgage company would go to the underwriter and say, "Hey, why did you approve this?" After being questioned about their decision, many underwriters would become gun-shy and going forward, would place absolutely absurd conditions on their loans to cover their asses.

One of the most nonsensical cases for Earl was actually a really solid case with a younger couple helping their mother buy a house. And in that case, he did an FHA loan because it was the most beneficial way to do it for the customer. It didn't require any additional down payment and the standards were liberal. It was called a non-occupant co-borrower situation, with a couple living in their own house and helping the mother buy a house for her to occupy. It was a perfect case. Both the mother and the young couple had perfect credit. The income was excellent, and the qualifying ratios were very low, which is good. They had lots of money in reserve. It was the perfect loan. However, the underwriter came back with two conditions.

One, she questioned a $27 deposit into their checking account. Earl confronted the underwriter and said, "You've got to be joking." And she said, "Nope." Earl had to call the man to address this issue. Thankfully, he was a really nice guy. Earl said, "Sir, I'm embarrassed to tell you this..." It turned out the guy ran a Boy Scout troop, and some kid bought a shirt that didn't fit, so he had to return it. For Earl, this point was the most frustrating part of the mortgage business: chasing money. In other words, if they saw a deposit from an unknown source going into a bank account, they always questioned where it came from. The rationale was that they may have borrowed money to get this money. And if they borrow the money, that means there is a payback, which means the qualifying ratios could be out of line because there's a loan they're not putting into the mix. But, in this particular case, this underwriter questioned a $27 deposit.

The underwriter's second condition was regarding the company the man worked for, a well-known defense contractor in Northern Virginia, SAIC. In fact, in Tysons Corner, the company's location, they had named a street after the company. The underwriter requested that Earl verify the existence of SAIC as a viable business. Earl responded, "Lady, what world do you live in? You want me to go to Tysons Corner and take a picture of the street that they named after SAIC? What would you like me to do?" That's an example of some of the ridiculousness that the Bugeaters had to deal with.

Another situation that came up often was when a customer owned a house that they would retain and rent out and buy a new one to live in. The borrower was required to submit a lease on the house to offset the monthly mortgage payment. Unfortunately, if the borrower could not find a tenant prior to the closing date or could not find a tenant to pay the amount needed to qualify, sometimes people in the industry would submit bogus leases. There was a standard Northern Virginia lease agreement they would use, mickey it up, and send it to the underwriter.

A funny thing happened to Eddie the Pec on this particular issue. The borrower had to get a lease on his existing property to qualify for the new loan. The tenant's name was Mr. Choi. They ended up naming this one "the Choi lease," and they actually hung it on the wall in the office. The guy took a piece of paper from a legal pad and just wrote, "I, James Choi, will rent this property for $600. Signed James Choi." That was the lease, and the underwriter accepted it. They put the paper in a frame on the wall—another notch in Eddie's Bugeater Award belt.

As the loan-securing journey is nearing the end, the underwriter has signed off on all conditions and deems the loan "clear to close." Now, the company can send the loan papers over to the title company so they can blend it with their paperwork and conduct the closing. That's the last piece of the puzzle. One of the loan officer's responsibilities was to inform the customers of how much money they needed to bring to the settlement. This amount should be very close to the amount disclosed on the Good Faith Estimate at the time of loan application. But again, that wasn't always the case. Just as Bow was known to present artificially low rates to the customer, he also provided artificially low Good Faith Estimates to secure the customer's business. For example, Bow would submit an estimate to the customer of $3,000 less than competitors vying for their business. Many borrowers would think they would save $3,000 by working with Bow. Then, of course, the costs are $3,000 more when they go to settlement than he had initially disclosed to them. Bow had perfected a song and dance as to why the costs had gone up. Even though they never bought the song and dance, the fact that the moving vans were already loaded up and ready to roll tended to make the borrower give in and sign the closing papers.

For settlements today, one hits a button, the whole PDF package is transmitted electronically, and the funds for closing are wired. In the old days, getting a courier to deliver the package on time wasn't always possible, so the loan officer would often drop what they were doing to deliver a hardcopy package to the settlement table along with a cashier's check. The buyer, seller, realtors for both sides and the title agent would be sitting around a table anxiously awaiting the arrival of the closing papers. The loan officer would proudly appear with the closing package and make it known that he or she had made this happen. And, as in the movies, the journey ended happily.

Chapter 13

An Equal Opportunity Membership

The Bugeaters' practice of preying upon and jerking around their customers was well documented. It was a customary and profitable way of life. However, it would be a mistake for one to assume that all of their energy was funneled in that one direction. As previously noted, whipping boy Ab La Sword was the focal point of considerable Bugeater aggression. But no member was safe, and all were fair game. The Clown Prince was a favorite target, given his proclivity for bullshitting anybody who would listen and an aura of abject foolishness. Even the Bugeater potentate, Chairman Eddie the Pec, was not exempt from internal hazing and tomfoolery.

Bow was so easy to fuck with it wasn't even funny. All of The Company loan originators carried voice pagers where one could leave a message that generated a signal that someone had called. Whenever Bow would spend the day at the strip club, golf course, or bowling alley, he would change his greeting to "Good afternoon. I am currently attending a VHDA seminar in Richmond and, therefore, cannot return your call immediately. Please leave a message, and I will call you back during normal business hours."

There were several problems inherent in Bow's voicemail message. The fact that it was on the pager at least once a week made one wonder how many seminars any institution could reasonably conduct and why one person would attend every single one of them. Further, it was puzzling to many realtors who contacted Bow about VHDA loans (Virginia Housing Development Authority) to be told The Company did not do VHDA loans (The Company, of course, did them, but Bow did not want to deal with them due to the tighter qualifying requirements, and therefore, extensive paperwork). When

An Equal Opportunity Membership

asked why he attended so many seminars on a product The Company did not offer, Bow responded that he wanted to be prepared for the day that they did. The other reason Bow didn't like VHDA loans was that the Commonwealth of Virginia set the price of the loan, which precluded loan originators and mortgage banking firms from making overage. Bow would steer any customers requesting a VHDA loan to another product in the interest of providing an enhanced profitable opportunity—a classic bait-and-switch move initiated by the Master himself.

Voice pagers are like any secure device in that they require a password to access the many functions available, such as recording a greeting. It became one of the great happenings in Bugeater lore when Earl discovered Bow's password—too good to be true, yet it was true. Earl wrote up a script and engaged the services of a young man working in the post-closing department. He used the password to break in and had his accomplice record a new greeting.

The following day, realtors and customers attempting to reach the Clown Prince were greeted with, "Good afternoon. I will be playing a round of golf today and do not wish to be disturbed. Anything you may be calling about can wait until I am available. Leave a number and message if you wish. Remember, patience is a virtue."

Of course, the shit hit the fan. Bow was in his customary drunken stupor in the early evening when the calls started to come in. Realtors, loan applicants, and even his girlfriend were appalled upon listening to his arrogant and condescending greeting. Before he passed out, he vowed to get to the bottom of this outrage.

Bow awoke the next morning hungover as always. He was fuming and determined to find out who was fucking with him. He decided to get to the office early to raise some hell. He walked in at 10:45 and immediately headed toward Johnny Gumba's office. Had his eyes not been burning and his head not pounding, he might have noticed the grins and laughter coming from all of the staff he encountered as he stumbled down to Johnny's office. Everybody at The Company knew what had happened, as Earl made a point of communicating to the world at large whenever Bow screwed up.

As Bow walked in, Gumba did his best not to break out in a fit of laughter.

"Johnny, you won't believe what these bastards did."

"What bastards?"

"Earl and Eddie."

"What did they do, and how do you know it was them?"

"Nobody else would do this. They broke into my pager and left a message that I was playing golf."

"Well, where were you?"

"Ah, well, I was playing golf."

"Why the hell weren't you making sales calls?"

"Johnny. I've been really hitting the streets hard. I need a break once in a while. Besides, these pricks cost me five million dollars of new business."

"Really? Five million? That's pretty good, considering you haven't done five million in the past three months."

"So, what are you gonna do about this crap?"

"What I'm going to do is tell you to get your hungover ass out on the street and get some loans. I've got a lot of bad habits to pay for."

So, once again, Bow tucked his tail between his legs and retreated to his office. As ticked off as he was, even he knew that he possessed neither the brains nor the guts to combat the Bugeater leadership. He hunkered down in his chair and stared at the ten unanswered phone messages that decorated the top of his desk. He did not turn his light on, which, in Bow's world, meant that he really wasn't there. What should he do? The same thing he did every Wednesday afternoon. Round up Tim and head down to the Camelot. There was a bumper crop of dancers every Wednesday, most of whom he was on a first-name basis with. On the way out of his office, he made sure to throw the phone messages in the trash can. That way, he wouldn't have to deal with them tomorrow.

The Bugeaters were ecstatic—another notch in their belt. Earl was especially gratified knowing that, once again, the Clown Prince was brought to his knees. He simply could not fathom how such a colossal screw-up could do the amount of business that he did. Nobody did less and got more out of it than Bow. Earl resented it and made it a Bugeater mandate to target Bow aggressively and often. Chairman Eddie agreed wholeheartedly.

Business was good. Daddy's well-oiled machine continued to get tons of loans in the door and out the door, which meant the cash register rang non-stop. When Johnny Gumba was promoted to manager, he had inherited a much-desired spacious corner office. After two years in the coveted space, a bigger office with a better view became available. Gumba asserted his authority and announced that henceforth he would oversee his fiefdom from that office. The scuttlebutt began. Who would get the corner office?

Like most salespeople, loan originators are great rivals with respect to their competition and within their own ranks. It cannot be emphasized enough how significant it was as to who would occupy the now vacant office.

A few days after Johnny moved up the hall, Columbo went to the vacant office to view the Telerate screen. Gumba had not had time to move it to his new office yet, so the loan officers continued showing up in the old office to get a gauge on the bond market that dictated where interest rates would be set. Upon entering the office, he encountered Eddie, who was behind the desk pulling on some phone wires.

"Eddie, what the hell are you doing in here?"

"My phone cord isn't working, so I'm going to replace it with one of these."

"To hell you are. I'm taking this office over. Leave the cord alone and everything else."

"You're what? Who said that? No way. Over my dead body."

"That's the way it is. Get over it."

Eddie stormed out. He couldn't believe it. He went to his office and seethed. He pulled out his resignation letter that he had dated so many times that one would almost need a drill to cut through all the whiteout that had built up.

Meanwhile, Columbo went to Earl's office to relay the story to him. They both laughed so hard they were almost crying. Earl said, "The only better thing you could have done would have been to tell him that I'm taking the office over. He'd crap in his pants."

Columbo was visibly excited. "That's awesome. Let's do it. I'll go to post-closing and drop the news. The whole company will know about it in ten minutes. I'll fill Johnny in because you know Eddie will be in there singin' the blues."

According to the script, within a half hour, Eddie was demanding to see Johnny Gumba. Gumba told his secretary to tell Eddie he was too busy to see him and that it would have to wait. Eddie was about to blow a gasket. After waiting ten minutes, he burst past the secretary and flew into Johnny's office. Gumba tried to maintain a straight face as he informed Eddie that he was trying to put out a bunch of fires and therefore had no time for him. Eddie stormed out and informed the grinning secretary that this was the last straw. He was going to get that son of a bitch, Earl.

To ease the pain, Eddie headed to the golf course. For the next four hours, he overwhelmed his partners with grousing and disillusionment about what was going on at The Company. His three partners couldn't wait to finish the round because they played golf for enjoyment and not to be engulfed by a cloud of negativity.

Eddie was heading home in the early evening when he decided he could not help himself. He detoured and headed directly to The Company. He hoped that, as was the norm, Johnny Gumba would still be there. He was rewarded when he saw Johnny's office light still on.

He stormed in and said, "John. We need to talk – now."

"I told you this afternoon I'm in the middle of a bunch of things that need immediate attention. What is so damn important that you need to interrupt me? This better be good."

"John. How could you do this to me? I've been here longer than Earl, and I've done more business than Earl. How can you give him that office?"

"Let me tell you something. A man in my position has to make many decisions every day. Earl has been a good employee and has done good business for this company. I had a decision to make, and I made it. My advice to you is focus on your own business and stop worrying about everybody else. This is the last I want to hear about this crap."

To say Eddie was furious was a gross understatement. He went home and wore out his wife by bitching and complaining. She went to bed early as she couldn't take any more. He sat up all night, trying to decide what to do next, exactly.

Meanwhile, Earl was having a jolly old time. He knew Eddie was beside himself and would be in rare form at the office tomorrow. He couldn't wait to get to work early and carry out the rest of the plan.

Earl showed up at 8:00 a.m. and went right to work. He moved his family pictures to the credenza in the corner office and put his loan files on the desk. He leaned his prints against the door to make it appear he would soon be hanging them on the walls of his new office. He then sat at his "new" desk and waited for Eddie to arrive. He did his best to refrain from bursting out in laughter.

At 8:30 a.m., Earl saw Eddie roll into the parking lot. Two minutes later, Eddie was flying up the hallway heading directly to the corner office. Earl picked up the phone and began a fake conversation with a fake customer. Eddie stood in front of the desk for five minutes as Earl carried on his bogus conversation. His face was beet red, and his blood pressure was through the roof. Earl finally hung up the phone and looked up at Eddie.

Eddie blasted him. "So. You're moving in here?"

Earl looked at the prints in the doorway and the files on his desk. "What does it look like to you?"

"This is bullshit. This is the last straw. I'm outta here." Eddie proceeded to approach all staff members who would listen to him. Of course, everybody but Eddie knew what was going on. They all sympathized with him and agreed he got royally screwed. It was like pouring gasoline on a fire.

Earl had convened the other Bugeaters in Columbo's office. They watched Eddie go from person to person to plead his case. It was belly laughs for everybody. The plan was to let him run until noontime and then take him to lunch and spill the beans.

Around 10:00 a.m., Earl and Columbo found out that Johnny Gumba had told Eddie what was going on. They went to his office and confronted Gumba.

Earl asked, "Why did you tell him, John? We were supposed to wait till lunchtime."

"Why did I tell him? Let me tell you why. My secretary told me he was sitting outside my office for fifteen minutes. I went out there, and he was sitting in a chair, staring at the floor. He wouldn't look up. He wouldn't talk. I thought he was going to jump off the balcony. I can't afford any suicides."

Of course, going forward, Eddie told everyone who asked that he knew what was going on the whole time. He was just playing along. This was totally par for the course.

The next week, Earl had rushed out to get a quick bite to eat and head back to the office. It was very busy, and he did not have the time for a lengthy Bugeater lunch. He came off the elevator and headed toward the desk of Missy, the receptionist, to retrieve any phone messages. Suddenly, he heard a voice cry out, "Earl! Earl!"

Earl looked over beyond the elevators and saw that it was Andrew, Daddy's driver and assistant, who had called out to him. With him was a gentleman of Hispanic descent who was visibly agitated as he spoke out loudly in Spanish. Andrew was waving to Earl to come over and quell the situation. Earl instinctively knew he wanted nothing to do with this situation, but he liked Andrew and did not want to ignore him.

Earl walked over, and Andrew introduced him to Hector. Hector was waving his arms and talking in a mixture of Spanish and English. He continuously muttered, "Salisbury."

"What's up, Andrew?" asked Earl.

"Hector is here for a refi with Reverend, but he didn't show up."

"Page him. I'm sure he's just running behind."

"We already paged him twice. He was supposed to be here an hour ago."

Earl looked at Hector and said, "You mentioned Salisbury. Do you mean Salisbury, Maryland?"

"Si."

"You traveled here from Salisbury, Maryland, for a refinance? That's three hours away."

"Si."

"Wow. All I can do is page Reverend again. I'm sure there's a good reason why he's not here." Earl didn't believe that was true, but he had to say something.

Hector shouted a few expletives in Spanish and jumped into the elevator.

Andrew shrugged his shoulders and headed to Daddy's office.

Earl approached Missy and asked, "L&N for lunch?"

"Yup. Bow dragged him out of here about an hour ago. They're probably at the bowling alley by now."

"Nice. Nobody can accuse those two of not having priorities. A pair to beat a full house."

Earl went to his office and worked on several loans that he had in play. He finished up around 6:00 p.m. and hit the gym. He relayed the Hector story to his workout partners, who were continuously amused and amazed by what Earl had to report on a daily basis. The $64,000 question was: How the hell did these people make a living?

Earl came in the next morning and greeted Missy as usual. She considered it a fringe benefit of her job that she got to witness the antics of the Bugeaters every day of the week. Earl was heading toward his office when the lightbulb came on. "Missy."

"Yeah?"

"When Reverend comes in, give it ten minutes and let him know that Hector is waiting in the lobby."

She burst out laughing. "Consider it done."

Earl assembled the troops in the office directly across from Reverend's. He walked in, and sure enough, the phone rang ten minutes later. When Reverend hung up, he looked like he had just seen a ghost. The boys were loving it. Reverend came out of his office and began to pace up and down.

Earl was laughing like hell when he said, "Watch this!" He walked out toward Reverend. "What's happening, Rev?"

He stuttered and stammered and finally got out, "Hector's out in the lobby."

"Hector? You mean that crazy Hispanic guy?"

"Yeah."

"Damn. He's got a bad temper. What are you going to do?"

"I dunno."

"You best face the music and go out there. But be careful!"

"Yeah, you're right. I should have shown up."

Reverend sauntered out to the lobby where a customer was waiting for Eddie. Reverend rushed up to him and cried out, "Hector. Hector. I'm so sorry. I got tied up. I'll make it up to you. I'll cut the loan fees. I'm so sorry."

The gentleman was aghast. "I'm Bob Smith. I don't know who Hector is, and I don't know who the hell you are. But get out of my face."

Reverend stepped back in shock. When he looked over at Missy and saw her laughing uncontrollably, he knew he'd been had once again. Strike one more for the Bugeaters. He'd be the laughingstock until the next fool came along.

In addition to being a mortgage banking superhero and an avid sports enthusiast, Eddie was also into politics. That drew him to a Bill O'Reilly book signing at Tysons Corner. While waiting in line to have Bill autograph his book, Eddie ran into Mark E., a mortgage banking colleague. It so happened that Mark E. was running for Congress, and he passed some campaign literature to Eddie. They exchanged pleasantries and went their separate ways. Eddie had always considered Mark E. to be a real flake and was not surprised he would make a run at Congress. In fact, Earl hired a loan processor who worked for him and continuously expressed her opinion that he didn't know his ass from his elbow. The next morning, Earl came in to find on his desk an invite to a campaign barbeque for Mark E., to which Earl was supposedly going to contribute $5,000. Earl sprung into action. He addressed an envelope to the Mark E. campaign headquarters and placed a one-dollar bill with the following letter to accompany the campaign contribution:

> Dear Mark,
>
> It was great to see you last evening. Even better to find out you are running for Congress. This country needs the kind of leadership that you can provide. Please accept my contribution to your dynamic campaign. I am also really interested in your views on the future of mortgage banking. Please call me at your convenience at 703-850-xxxx.
>
> Yours in mortgage banking,
> Eddie

The call came the next day when Eddie was riding down Route 66. For once in his life, Eddie was speechless. Mark E. tore him a new one. "I don't have time for this, and my staff doesn't either. Who do you think you are? This is serious business. I am trying to make this a better country." (His staff consisted of his wife.)

Chapter 14

Underwriters aka The Wizard of Oz?

There's always been a mystical attitude about underwriters because there's one thing that's totally forbidden in the mortgage business: customers cannot call up a mortgage company and speak to an underwriter. It's absolutely taboo. So now a mystical creature is going to make the biggest decision in a person's financial life: whether or not they can buy this house. And they can't converse with the person because everything's funneled through somebody else. So, it's like *The Wizard of Oz,* with this guy behind a curtain pulling a bunch of levers.

Anybody in the mortgage industry and perhaps in the real estate industry, too, will understand some of the lyrics to this song. Other people may not, but it's easily explained. The title of the song is "We lost Direct Endorsement," and it's sung to the tune of "You've Lost That Lovin' Feeling" by The Righteous Brothers.

> You should close your eyes when you take a look at this loan.
> And for old times' sake, can you not throw me a bone?
> You're trying hard not to do it, Daddy, but Daddy, Daddy approve it!!!
> We lost direct endorsement,
> we lost direct endorsement,
> we lost direct endorsement,
> Now it's gone gone gone, whoa whoa whoa.
>
> Daddy, Daddy, I'll get down on my knees for you.
> If you would only close them like you used to do.

> You lost DE, DE, you let it slip away.
> Now don't, don't, don't lose VA.
> Daddy, Daddy, now bring it on back,
> bring it on back, bring it on back.
> We lost direct endorsement,
> we lost direct endorsement,
> we lost direct endorsement.
> Now it's gone, gone, gone, whoa whoa whoa.

When a loan officer is doing an FHA loan, if the company has direct endorsement, they can underwrite that loan as the lender. If the company doesn't have direct endorsement, they must send the loan to FHA for underwriting, which adds thirty more days to the process. So, it was a big deal. With VA, they called it "VA Automatic," which means the lender can underwrite the loan versus sending it to VA, which goes into a black hole, and God knows when it would come out.

In today's world, they have what they call "automated underwriting," and Fannie Mae and Freddie Mac have their own systems where the loan data is entered into the computer, and it comes back and says, "Yay" or "Nay." Back in the Bugeater era, the underwriters had a lot more discretion and had to make all those decisions on their own. For example, there was no credit scoring back then. There was a credit report. The underwriters had to go line by line to see if there were any problems and, if there were, determine how big a problem was. That's a huge difference. With the qualifying ratios, there were always two ratios to be considered. There's the monthly housing expense divided by the income. That was called the front-end ratio. The back ratio was the housing expense plus any other fixed obligations divided by the income. If the ratios exceeded what the program called for, the underwriter had discretion. For example, if the ratios were three points higher than allowed, but the borrower had tons of money left over after closing, and their credit history was flawless, the underwriter could use those reasons to justify the loan approval. But these days, it's strictly the computer's decision, so if the computer says, "No," it's "No."

There is a huge difference between underwriting with a credit report versus credit scores, which did not exist back then. For example, many loans require a credit score of 700 for approval today. A 695 is not going to fly. Since there is only a five-point difference, many loan officers would try to do a re-score by getting the person to pay off a credit card and then re-pull the score and hope it goes over 700. But with credit scoring and the automated underwriting, it's pretty clear-cut. The computer is telling you, and the credit score is telling you either this loan is going to work or it's not. Back in the day, the underwriter, the mystical figure, had to actually look at all this stuff, scrutinize it, and determine whether or not they would let this thing fly. If there were late payments on the credit report, the underwriter would have to consider how recent and numerous they were. It is interesting to note that it seems like anyone who had a Sears credit card had at least one late payment on it. No one knows why. That's just a fact. If there were late payments, the loan officer would tell the customer they must write a credit letter and explain why they were late on their AMEX account or Sears account card, which led to some great stories. And some of the credit letters that they got were off the rails.

Reverend had a female customer with perfect credit, except for one month. So, he did the standard thing, called her, and said, "Hey, I see these late payments for May 1991, and I need you to explain that in writing so I can submit it to the underwriter." And she said, "Oh, okay." So, the woman wrote a letter saying that she broke up with a boyfriend and moved to Florida because she couldn't deal with the depression. And then, after she moved down there, the boyfriend showed up. And they spent the next month making passionate love. And she wrote, "I could think nothing of anything else except for him. And then the son of a bitch packed up and headed back to Northern Virginia. So, I came back and realized that I was late, and then I paid my bills."

Earl got a credit letter that was so good they had to frame it and put it up on the wall. It involved a gentleman with the typical one-time late payment on a Sears credit card three years prior. Earl called him up to say he needed to explain this dire credit situation. The gentleman said he'd be happy to and sent the following letter: "Let me explain to you why I was late once in my lifetime. I actually wrote the check out to Sears and put it in the envelope. And I took it out to my mailbox to mail it. But a gust of wind blew the letter down into a ravine near my home. So, I went down into the ravine, and I actually heard gunfire. And it turns out that we were being besieged by terrorists. So, first, I had to hunker down, and then I had to escape the neighborhood and hide out for a few days. And when I came back, I realized that I'd never made the payment. So, I finally sent that in, and I guess, apparently, it was late. So, I'm sorry about that."

Earl remembers another time when somebody wrote a letter that said, "I forgot to mail the payment." The one and only time, someone told the truth.

Many loan officers had template letters. They would use these forms to write the letter for the customer and put their name on it. They would have a template to suit different types of situations. For example, "I need a template C on this one," so they fired it up and put the name on it. The realtors who were representing the people buying the house wanted to make sure they got that commission, so they had their own letters, too. They'd say, "I'll write the letter and get it to you." The whole thing was so absurd because if someone is late once or twice, is it that serious? And why do you need somebody to make up a reason?

Earl had a couple who came in for a loan application. They were boyfriend and girlfriend, not married, but they planned to buy the house together and live there. The male had very bad credit. So, Earl couldn't put him on the loan. Therefore, the female would be on the loan by herself. On her own, she was borderline approvable. The gentleman had a good job with a big-time company and made good money but had bad credit.

So, Earl bolstered the file by having the man submit some pay stubs to show what kind of money he made and write a letter saying, "I'm not technically on this loan, but I'm going to live in the house and contribute to the housing payment, and please see that I make X amount of money per month."

So, they approved the loan, and it closed. Somehow, the loan ended up on Daddy's desk, who questioned, "Hey, how did this loan get approved? Is Earl screwing the underwriter?"

Four months later, Daddy's assistant, Mr. Z, calls Earl into the office and says, "Hey, can you tell me something about this?"

And Earl said, "What am I going to tell you?"

Mr. Z said, "Well, perhaps you could tell me why they haven't made a payment in four months."

And Earl says, "Whoa, I had no idea. I'll look into it." So, Earl calls the female. He remembered she was a manager at a Red Lobster restaurant; nice lady. "Hey, can you tell me why you haven't made a payment in four months?" And then he could feel the air being sucked out of the telephone.

She says, "Oh, my God. Yeah. We closed the loan, and we were going to move in, and then we got into a big fight. I agreed to let him move into the house under the promise that he would make the payments. And then I moved to an apartment." And, of course, he didn't make the payments. She made good on it, ponied up for four months, and got it right.

As documented in the Bow chapter, if he had a customer with the typical Sears card late payment, he would contact them and say, "Oh, we have a big problem here. I'm going to see if I can get the committee to take care of this." And then he'd come back inevitably and say, "Yeah, I got them to do it. But we have to add a point to the loan." And, of course, the customer was so freaked out by then they said that was fine with them. They just wanted to close the loan. There is more about this concept of adding points in the marketeering chapter.

Then there was the concept of what they called no-doc, low-doc loans, and no-income loans. These loans existed back in 1987 when Earl first got into the business, and he was amazed. He tried to understand what was happening. "You're telling me that you're gonna let people get this loan, but you're not gonna verify their income?" That was correct. It was based on whether the person had real good credit or they had a lot of money, which eliminated the requirement to verify income. The rationale for these loans was that they were mostly for self-employed people because if they submitted their tax returns, they would not show enough qualifying income due to the nature of writing off the maximum expenses to reduce taxable income. Underwriting would have to take the gross revenue, subtract the expenses, and only use the net income for qualifying. Many self-employed people write off more expenses than they should, which means that the net qualifying income isn't going to fly. People were abusing this situation, and in the industry, these loans became known as "liar loans." Even though they weren't going to verify the income, the person still had to put it on a loan application. The loan officer would say, "How much money do you make?" or "How much money did you make last year?" And the customer would say, "Well, what do you need?"

There is a great story Earl tells about a guy in the industry. He wasn't one of the Bugeaters, but they all knew him; everybody in the industry knew everybody. So, the Washington Post wrote a story about these no-doc, low-income, no-income, no-nothing, loans. And they interview this guy, and he says, "I got a guy flipping burgers at McDonald's, and I put down he makes eighty grand a year." So, they print this article, and the shit hits the fan. The management of the company comes down and says, "What are you doing?" He says, "Oh, no, no, I was taken out of context. I meant Burger King." That was an actual event.

In the Bugeater era, there was always this thing of "common sense underwriting." When a loan originator was going to interview with a new mortgage company, during the interview, they were always told, "Oh, we have common sense underwriting." What exactly does that mean? It's just a BS term.

Eddie had one of the great low-doc loans of all time. His borrower was a military guy, an Officer, an O-3. The way the designations work in the US Army, O-3 is a Captain. Then O-4 is a Major, O-5 is a Lieutenant Colonel, and O-6 is a Colonel. Everybody in the United States can go and pull up a military pay chart and know this borrower's income. This guy's buying a house at least four times the price he should be buying. And somehow, Eddie thinks he's going to pull this off, right? So, he submits it. Somehow, they found a bank that booked this loan. And they actually closed it.

There were different variations of these "liar loans." For example, you could have a no-income loan and still need to verify assets. A no-doc loan means not verifying anything, no assets, no income, basically pulling a credit report, and if it meets the standard, then they make the loan. With these loans, they charge higher interest rates because there's more risk associated with them.

But getting back to the nature of underwriters, Reverend frequently clashed with this head underwriter. She would look at a file, and if it was Reverend's, she would page him, and then he'd call back. And she would say, "You know, I don't feel comfortable with this file."

And Reverend would say, "Well, lady, we're not paying you to be comfortable with this file. Either sign off on it or don't sign."

Inevitably, it would end up on Daddy's desk. Then he'd call Reverend in, take a quick look at it, and say, "Fair to say that you did not do a good job on this file, Rev?"

Reverend would confirm, saying, "Yeah, that's fair. That's a fair statement."

Then Daddy would hem and haw and finally say, "I'm gonna sign off on this thing, but get the hell out of here and go get some more loans."

Many times, underwriters came up with foolish conditions because they were running scared; they didn't want to take the risk. There was a fine line for the underwriter to walk. If she was turning loans over to Daddy that she should be approving, at some point, he's going to say, "Lady, what's going on here? You're not doing your job." But on the other side of that coin, if they signed off on loans that went bad, then Daddy would come back and say, "Hey, you signed off on this, and it's costing us X amount of money." Underwriters walked a fine line.

There was no financial liability for the underwriter signing off on a loan that went into default. They were employees, so one time would not get anyone fired, but if there was a consistent pattern, one could lose their job.

The mortgage banking game worked a certain way, and Daddy was so successful because he knew how the game worked. It was a very busy time, with billions of dollars of loans getting funneled into Fannie Mae, Freddie Mac, FHA, and VA. Daddy was walking a fine line, too. The company did so well because the real estate community knew that Daddy would close a loan if there were any possible way to do so. He was playing a numbers game. For example, if he had one hundred loans and took some risks on some of them and one of them went bad, he could sell that loan to an investor at maybe 60 to 70 cents on the dollar. He took a loss, but the 99 other loans made up for it. They'd lose one hand, but they got 99 other good ones. They were making money hand over fist. That was the game.

An interesting story about Direct Endorsement (DE) featured Johnny Gumba, who got certified for his DE, which meant he could sign off on FHA loans. That was tantamount to the fox sitting on the roof of the hen house. And his first question to the loan officer was, "How much money do you have in this loan?" There will be more about overages in the next chapter; an overage means the loan officer is charging the customer more than the actual price of the loan. So, if Johnny got an FHA loan to underwrite and there was more profit in the loan than there normally would be, he'd just take the pen out, sign that thing, and fire it down the road. That was his deal, just the way he did things, similar to how Bow had this fictitious committee he told customers he sent their loans to when there was no committee. So, for Johnny, if the loan officer had enough profit in the loan, this was, in essence, the Johnny Gumba committee. He would sign off on it and just move on.

As part of the underwriting process, the underwriters also had to underwrite the appraisal. Independent appraisers did the appraisals, but underwriters had to review each one to make sure that they were following the guidelines and they were not stepping out of line.

Appraisals are a funny thing, and in sellers' markets, people are willing to pay way over the list price for homes. Normally, when a house is priced, whether it's by the realtors or their appraiser, they work on comparables. Typically, three comparable properties are used to establish the price of the house, but if you have three comparables that say the house is worth $600,000, prospective buyers often bid up the price, which could become $690,000, for example. It's essentially Economics 101, supply and demand. It's what happens when there is little inventory and many buyers. So, the $64,000 question is, how in the hell did that house appraise for $690,000? Somehow, it does.

One of the craziest things that ever happened to Earl was when he was doing a loan down in what they call the Northern Neck of Virginia, heading to the Chesapeake Bay toward Virginia Beach. It's very rural country there. The subject property had 25 acres with a farmhouse on it and a cottage and a barn. It was hard to get comparables for a refinance loan, so Earl asked the owner, "What do you think this house is worth?" because he had a better sense of that area than Earl. The owner said that $650,000 sounded reasonable. Earl sent the appraiser out there. He comes back with a value of $300,000. Earl figures either this appraiser or the owner is smoking something. Normally, lenders don't like to get two appraisals, but Earl said, "Look at this. Something is wrong." So, they ended up getting a second appraisal. And sure enough, it came in at $650,000. Appraisers are like anybody else: the good, the bad, and the mediocre.

Eddie had a borrower who wanted to get a loan on a house. Earl still has a picture of the house somewhere. Eddie was trying to get an appraiser to appraise this house that looked like somebody put a bomb in it. The roof tiles and wires were hanging down and the ceiling inside the house was basically gone. The walls were punched in, it was just unbelievable. And Eddie just couldn't understand why no appraiser would touch it. The Bugeaters were laughing and saying, "Are you joking?" At the end of the day, Eddie was just trying to make a deal.

One morning, Reverend was at the office early, trying to deal with a situation where an appraisal had come in low. Coincidentally, the realtor team (husband and wife) involved in the transaction showed up unannounced to voice their disapproval of the low appraisal. They were dressed like a couple you would see at a C-grade casino out in Reno, Nevada. The guy had a Rhinestone Cowboy hat, cowboy boots, and one of those little tie-clasp things with this funky suit coat. The wife had cowboy boots and an Annie Oakley kind of skirt.

Daddy came rolling into the office fresh off three hours of sleep from the night before. He saw these characters in the lobby and called Reverend, who was extremely nervous, into the office and said, "What are these people doing here? Who are these people?"

"Well, they're my agents."

Daddy responds, "What are they doing here?"

"Well, they don't like your appraisal."

Daddy said, "So, they don't like my appraisal, huh? Let me take care of this." He shooed Reverend out and brought the couple in.

As the Rhinestone Cowboy entered the door of Daddy's office, he said in his drawl, "Well, looks like y'all don't want to do any loans around here."

Daddy was a proud man who had built the premier company in the area, and he was not amused. He informed the couple he would review the appraisal and make the appraiser get it right. At that point, he was just happy to get those two rubes out of his office.

Earl has another appraisal story involving a refinance in a big condo project in Arlington where there was actually a real estate office housed within the condo development. Legally, they were condos but physically, townhomes. Earl did a lot of business down there.

One day, he had a realtor refer a couple to him who wanted to refinance their condo unit. So, Earl sent one of The Company's usual appraisers to the home. Before he sent in the appraisal report, in the middle of talking to him about something else, Earl said, "Hey, how'd that appraisal go down in Arlington?"

The appraiser started laughing and said, "It was scheduled for 11 o'clock on a Tuesday. I get there and knock on the door. And nobody answers the door. So, I keep knocking, and finally, I hear this voice. 'Hey, come on in.' So, I go in, and I'm in the foyer and don't see anybody, so I'm calling, 'Hello, hello.' I hear this guy calling, 'Come on in here.' I walk into the bedroom. And here's this guy sitting in bed with his girlfriend, stark naked with the covers on, smoking a cigarette. And he says, 'Hey, how are you doing? Want to look around?' And I said, 'Yeah, I guess." Earl tells the story as just the normal everyday occurrence in the mortgage business. And the appraisal came back fine.

A funny story from when Earl first started in the business, and he and Mr. Miller (Bugeater Treasurer) worked together. They were at the lender where Earl started out before moving on to The Company with all the Bugeaters. Being new to the business, Earl was trying to do everything by the book. This was his first FHA loan, which, in those days, was kind of complicated. You would start with the borrower's gross income and then utilize Federal and State withholding tax charts to come up with a net income. Utility charts based on the square footage of the home were used to calculate the utility expense. The final net income would have to meet the FHA residual income charts for the size of the family. So, Earl got all his tax charts out, did his due diligence, dotted every I and crossed every T, and got the loan submitted to underwriting.

The underwriter came back and denied the loan.

Earl, just starting in the business with his first FHA loan, is ready to jump off a cliff. So, he called Mr. Miller and said, "Hey, look, I did all the steps to calculate the residual. And then they denied my loan. How do you do yours?"

He said, "I just eyeball it."

Earl says, "What?!"

A long story short, the underwriter had made a mistake. And then they corrected it and finally closed the loan for Earl, but, yeah, "I just eyeball it."

And then the last thing was the great Johnny Gumba underwriting story. A basic rule of underwriting is that you must show two years of employment history. Let's say a person graduated from college and has been on a job for a year. That's okay because underwriters will count the college time as employment, and you're meeting the two-year requirement. A loan was submitted where only six months of employment history was verified. The underwriter asked where the borrower worked previously, and he said he was in Federal prison before getting his job six months earlier. To say the underwriter was not comfortable with this situation was an understatement. So, she took the loan to Gumba. The fact that the borrower was in Federal prison in and of itself did not deter Gumba, because Johnny, as previously mentioned, had done some time at taxpayer's expense himself. All he wanted to know was, what was the guy in for? If it was some kind of theft, he wasn't going to approve the loan because he figured, well, "Then he's going to try to rip me off," but if it was something else, like selling coke or something like that, it would be acceptable. That was his rationale.

Chapter 15

The Drawer:
Mini-Marketeers and Pocket Locks

More so than any other, the subject of this chapter requires a detailed explanation. Most people are not even aware of this part of the business and certainly won't understand some terminology if not defined. Hence, a comprehensive description of it is essential to understand what the hell these characters are talking about.

This song, written by the Bugeaters, is called "Lying in the Drawer," sung to the tune of "Blowing in the Wind."

> How many loans must an LO submit before he gets one approved?
> And how many deals will he take on the float before the market will move?
> The answer, my friend, is lying in the drawer.
> The answer is lying in the drawer.
> How many loans will he throw at the wall before he gets one to stick?
> And how many points will he add to their price before they call him a prick?
> The answer, my friend, is lying in the drawer.
> The answer is lying in the drawer.

What's the drawer? The drawer was Johnny Gumba's desk drawer. Normally, in the mortgage industry, a loan is registered when a lender takes in a loan application. At that point, the interest rate can be locked or allowed to float; it's the customer's choice. If they choose to lock the interest rate, they are protected from rate changes during the loan process (unless the Clown Prince decides to reach into his bag of tricks). Or, they may choose to float the interest rate, hoping the rates will go lower. Prior to Gumba joining The Company, the loan officers would take in a loan and register it. Upon Gumba becoming branch manager, he declared, "No, no, no, that's not what we're gonna do. I want you to write down all the information regarding this loan on a piece of paper and put it in this drawer. I'm going to play the market with it and decide when they get locked in."

One thing to understand here is there are a lot of levels of float in this business. For example, the loan officer could take the loan in and decide to float it himself in an effort to enhance his profit on the loan. And many people did that. Gumba set up the drawer because he wanted to control the float. But then Daddy, who's running The Company, has a secondary marketing department, and they can also float it. It was a very interesting concept.

Imagine if some of these customers found out that their loans were sitting in Johnny Gumba's desk drawer. If he guessed right and the market rolled down, there would be more profit for him and The Company. As noted, the offshoot of the drawer and the clear intent was to make more money for The Company and for the loan originators. In line with Gumba's desire to control the lock and float process, he created what was called the point bank. How did the point bank work?

Normally, if the loan officer had extra profit in the loan, it would be paid out along with the regular commission. When the point bank was instituted, all extra profits were held in the point bank, like a piggy bank. Gumba would pay out the point banks quarterly, referring to it as a "bonus." There were two ways to increase your point bank with overages.

One, take the loan in, and the market improves before it's locked. Now, there's more profit in the loan than before, hence creating an overage. Bow the Clown Prince was a master of this second method.

For example, if the price on the loan is 4% with one point, he'd charge 4% with two points. A point is 1% of the loan amount. That is the price he would quote the customer upfront. These were the two typical ways to increase your point bank.

Bow also used another more uncommon method to increase his overage. Midway through the loan process, as mentioned previously, he would create the fictitious credit issue, which would require "loan committee" approval, and a week later, he would announce the great news that the committee approved the loan with the addition of one point. Most customers were so relieved to get loan approval they didn't make an issue of it. And the few who did make an issue also realized they were boxed in with only a few days till settlement.

There is, of course, the other side of the coin. The market could go the wrong way, creating an underage when the loan is locked. The reality is, if you're going to play the bond market, it is similar to playing the stock market, where it could go up, down, or sideways.

It is duly noted there are many characters in this business. Some would take a loan in and not even pay any attention to it; they would just let it ride till two days before settlement. And whatever the price was at the time, they locked it in whether they took an overage or an underage. Mortgage rates follow the bond market because they're tied to the prices of the 10-year treasury bond. So, when someone is following the bond market and trying to determine which way rates will go, they are hoping that the market goes up. It's an inverse relationship. If the market is up, rates are down. If the market is off or down, rates are up. Most people know much more about the stock market than the bond market. To be clear, this is all about the bond market. The borrower assumes that when they are quoted 4% and one point, and they request that it be locked in, that it is, in fact, locked in at that price. And unless some other crazy stuff goes on, that will be the rate they'll get at settlement. As noted in the previous chapter, when they sit down at the loan application, they are given what's called a lock-in agreement.

For example, it says the rate is 4% with one point and is good until November 15. The loan will close on November 10. Everything else noted here is under the table. The customer has no idea about the drawer or point banks, overage or underage, and that's one of the reasons the authors wanted to write this book, to show people what went on behind the scenes before the legislation was passed that prevented many of these practices from continuing.

Now there are no more overages in the mortgage business. All that went away. From a 30,000-foot view, it's probably the right thing. However, it's interesting how they can impose that upon one industry but not others, such as the car industry or the personal loan industry. If the price of a car is $15,000 and somebody comes in, and they really want that car, they say, "How much is this car?" and are told, "It's $16,000," there's no regulation on that. There also doesn't seem to be any regulation on interest rates tied to personal loans that can charge more than forty percent these days.

Earl used to tell Johnny Gumba all the time, "Somebody's got to write a book about the underbelly of this business," and Gumba said, "Great idea, but just wait till we get out of the business." They wouldn't want someone reading these accounts thinking that these shenanigans are still going on behind the scenes, for example, loans in the desk drawer.

Okay, back to the way it was. Some of these guys would register the loan as floating and just wait until right before settlement to lock it in. They were doing two things: they wanted to play the market and let it ride. But the other thing to keep in mind is that the longer or shorter they lock in a loan, the worse or better the price they get. In other words, the 60-day lock will be more expensive than a 45-day lock, which is more expensive than a 30-day lock, which is more expensive than a 15-day lock. So, if they can ride it down to 15, they will still benefit from the shorter lock period, even if the market doesn't totally go their way. That's all part of that strategy. So, now for some stories.

The first story is about Earl and pocket locks. Earl had a gentleman come in one day for a loan application, a government worker, nice guy.

While taking the application, they got to the point of talking about the rate and whether to lock it in, and the guy says, "What's the rate now?"

Earl says, "It's four percent with one point."

"Okay. Yeah, let's go with that." While Earl is writing up the paperwork, the guy looks at him and says, "By the way, are you going to pocket lock me?"

Earl almost fell off the chair because he'd never heard that term before. He was asking Earl if he was going to put it in his pocket and ride the market for a while. So, Earl started laughing and said, "Well, I don't know, do you think I should?"

It was funny, and they both started laughing because he knew the game, but he was the one out of a hundred who knew it. Hence, pocket locks became a common term amongst the Bugeaters.

Then there is the character, Colombo. Usually, when they went out to make sales calls in the morning, it would be about 11 o'clock. At nine o'clock, the markets opened up, including the bond market. The Company had Telerate screens, like a TV, for reading the bond market. On this particular day, when Earl was heading out to his best account about 10:30 a.m., the market was way up. So, everybody was thinking, "Oh, this is great, we're gonna make some money." So, Earl got to the real estate office at about 11:15. He gets a page telling him the bond market is blowing up, it's way, way off. First thing, Earl is thinking somebody is jerking him around because it was up when he left. But it was true. So, Columbo was holding several loans, and the market just completely tanked through the day and finished way off, so now he's way the hell underwater. His strategy was, that's all right, I'll ride it out and get it back tomorrow. Nine o'clock the next morning, it blew up again. So finally, he had to surrender. He went to Daddy's office and pulled out the white flag. He was $60,000 in the tank. Daddy was going to fire him, obviously. But some of the Bugeaters talked to Daddy and somehow convinced him to keep Columbo, which turned out for the best. He was a good producer. And he learned these lessons: Not to play the market, and there were no secrets at The Company – everybody knew what happened. To say that Columbo was embarrassed was a gross understatement.

Now for the Tim story. They always said Tim was dangerous, but he didn't know that he was dangerous, and that's why he was dangerous. So, Tim takes in a VHDA loan, the strictly regulated Virginia State bond program. It's tailored to first-time buyers, and the state sets the interest rate. VHDA required two registrations, one with The Company and one with VHDA. And again, they set the rate. So good ol' Tim takes in a loan, doesn't register it with the state, and decides he will to try to take an overage on it, which is impossible because the state sets the rate. So, the loan goes all the way up to settlement. And then the shit hits the fan. Because, of course, the market had gone the other way. Big brother Johnny Gumba was beyond incensed. It goes without saying that he dressed down Tim at the next loan officer meeting. This classic example demonstrates how somebody wins a Mortgage Banker of the Year Award.

Here is another vintage Bow story. So, on this particular day, Earl walked by the copy room, where there was a big copying machine for the staff to copy original documents. Of course, Bow wouldn't make copies of documents; he'd make the customers copy them. Who does that? A couple is in the copy room making their copies, and Bow is sitting there, daydreaming.

To rile Bow up, Earl walks by the copy room and yells in, "Hey, I just heard on WMAL that the rates are plummeting! Whatever you do, don't lock your loan in!"

So, Bow freaks out. He starts blocking and pushing the people toward the back of the room so they can't hear Earl. But it was too late.

The husband called out, "What was that again? What was it, sir? What was that?"

Earl said, "Yeah, just turn on WMAL, the rates have plummeted. Whatever you do, don't lock your loan in."

Now, of course, Bow had already told him the loan was locked. He was furious and attempted to diffuse the situation. He told the couple, "Don't listen to this guy. He doesn't know what he's talking about."

Earl continued walking down the hall with a huge grin, knowing that, once again, Bow was on the ropes.

Reverend wouldn't be Reverend without having his own marketeering story. Every day, the Bugeaters assembled at the office, and one of the first things they did was look at the Telerate screen to see what the bond market was doing. Certain economic indicators, such as employment numbers, affect the bond market in different ways. These indicators usually come out on a Friday.

On a Wednesday, Reverend comes into the office and says, "Hey, guys, we're gonna kick ass on Friday. I know a guy with the Bureau of Labor Statistics who knows the employment number before it comes out. So, I'm going to get the number from him, and that'll tell us which way the market's gonna go."

The Drawer: Mini-Marketeers and Pocket Locks

So, they come into the office on Friday, and everybody's been holding loans because, according to Reverend, they think the market will be way up, leading to huge profits. It's getting close to 9 o'clock when the bond market opens, and Reverend is rubbing his hands together and says, "Boys, we're going to make a lotta money today."

Nine o'clock comes, and the market goes right down the hill. Nine o'clock is also the deadline for locking loans, so the Bugeaters were shut out, and they tearfully watched their commissions go down the drain.

The red-faced Reverend was rendered speechless as the Bugeaters demanded to know how this government genius could get this so wrong. "Well, it wasn't exactly a guy from the Bureau of Labor Statistics."

The next logical question was, "Could you perhaps tell us who it was?"

"It was my auto mechanic. He just told me the rates are gonna come down on Friday." Reverend had, once again, built a strong case for a Mortgage Banker of the Year award.

Most of the time, it's a daily roller coaster with the bond market, up one day and down the next. In October 1992, the rates were falling every single day. Nobody locked a loan during the first half of the month, even though business was booming. Johnny Gumba was staring at the drawer, wondering why it was empty every day. At the same time, Daddy was notified by Secondary Marketing that no loans had been locked for two weeks. Daddy called a meeting and wanted to know what the hell was going on. He let it be known that this situation better get straightened out, and he wanted to see loan registrations ASAP. After he left, it was almost like the Bugeaters were playing poker. One guy with ten loans was willing to throw in an FHA streamline. Another guy was willing to throw a couple of smaller loans into the pot, and then somebody else ponied up a small VA rate reduction. The bigger the loan, the more the profit, so they were willing to throw in the small loans to appease Daddy even though they were sure he knew what was going on.

As previously noted, Columbo got into hot water for holding several loans, and then there was the Eddie the Pec situation. The good news is he was only holding one loan, but the bad news was it was a real big one. He employed the same strategy as Columbo, thinking that when the market was off, he'd get it back the next day. He rolled the dice for three days, but the market never came back. He finally capitulated and locked the loan with a loss of $35,000. He thought he was going to get fired. Most mortgage companies would fire him without hesitation. But because he was doing good production, Gumba forgave him and just wrote off the loss.

Contrary to the popular belief that all of Bow's rate sheets ended up in the dumpster, some did, in fact, end up in real estate offices. However, the rates portrayed on these sheets bore no semblance to reality. In other words, the rates were totally fictitious. They were anywhere from a point to a point-and-a-half lower than the competition.

If a customer had Bow's rate sheet in hand and called him to lock the advertised rate, he'd say, "Oh, rates went up ten minutes ago." A classic bait-and-switch. As previously mentioned, a Washington Post article that focused on bait-and-switch artists like Bow, the Clown Prince.

It was so bad that, at one point, a real estate broker called up Johnny Gumba and said, "Hey, tell this clown not to come into my office anymore. He's putting rates out there that nobody in town is even remotely close to."

So, Gumba had to tell Bow, "Hey, you can't go in there anymore." The account was re-assigned to Ab La Sword. The first time Ab went into the account, a realtor confronted him, wanting to know when Bow was coming back in with his blue plate special.

As previously noted, the bond market would open up at 9 o'clock daily. The Company wouldn't put out the rate sheets until 11 o'clock. The Company's loan officers wanted to go out on the street earlier to distribute rate sheets. It was brought to Daddy's attention, so he directed Eskimo to deal with it. His way of dealing with it was to walk around the office each morning, snapping his fingers and saying, "Morning prices up a quarter." He did this 364 out of 365 days in the year. He was simply hedging the bet. Raising the price every morning meant that The Company couldn't really get hurt. The one day when the bond market was up two points, even Eskimo knew he couldn't get away with saying the rates were up a quarter, so he said, "Prices are even." That was also the one day he didn't snap his fingers.

Many loan officers considered themselves mini-marketeers and adept at playing the market. Sometimes it worked well; sometimes it didn't. Johnny Gumba and the Bugeaters took this role to a new level. The cash register never stopped ringing.

Chapter 16

The Company:
A Human Resources Nightmare

Anyone who has taken high school chemistry will be familiar with the concept of mixing different components with the goal of creating something. Chemists are experts who know that when you mix this with that you are going to get this. So, had a chemist created The Company and mixed large amounts of money, good-looking women, cocky loan originators, booze, and drugs, the result was entirely predictable – a human resources nightmare.

Daddy was fortunate that in The Company's early days, the concept of sexual harassment was also in its infancy. Of course, the behavior that came to be known as sexual harassment has existed forever. It was just that women were beginning to realize their rights and had started to exercise them. One could say that Daddy was like a chemist who had put The Company together and was fully cognizant of the combustible mix he had created. Being a "man's man" and knowing full well that "boys will be boys," he treated sexual harassment as a necessary evil. He didn't condone it, but he knew it was inevitable.

Mary Ann was The Company's Human Resources Director. She was a grandmotherly type who had graduated from Smith College many moons ago. She abhorred many of the goings-on but was deathly afraid of Daddy. Every day she wondered daily whether he would pull the plug on her. The Bugeaters, especially Eddie the Pec, represented everything she found reprehensible. Therein lay her problem. The Bugeaters were The Company's cash cow. And Mary Ann and everyone else knew it.

The Company: A Human Resources Nightmare

The Company was making money hand over fist. But they would have been out of business within the year if faced with the litigious environment of twenty-five years in the future imposed on perpetrators of sexual harassment in the workplace. That was basically the way Mary Ann viewed the situation. Daddy had a different point of view. Especially since one of the biggest perpetrators was Johnny Gumba himself.

The pattern of sexual harassment was fairly consistent. A male employee, ofttimes in a supervisory position, took up with a female employee. God knows what they may have promised to get them into bed, but it worked more often than not. After a couple of sexual encounters, the male would decide to move on, perhaps to a different employee, which did not typically sit well with the initial female. Often, the female would complain to her colleagues first and then bring her case to Mary Ann. In turn, Mary Ann went to Daddy. Mary Ann would try to relay the facts of the case and emphasize the seriousness of the situation, but it fell on deaf ears. Daddy would pull out his check book and stroke a $5,000 check to the aggrieved female. He would then order Mary Ann to convene a company meeting and once again hand out the redated harassment memorandum. The memo read as follows:

Memorandum
The Company

To: All employees
From: Mary Ann
Subject: Harassment
Date: November 22, 1993

It is the policy of The Company to prohibit sexual harassment of its employees in the workplace by any person, in any form, and to maintain a working environment free of sexual harassment, intimidation, or exploitation, either physical or verbal.

Each employee has a responsibility to create an environment free of sexual coercion and unwanted conduct. Examples of conduct considered sexually harassing and subject to discipline under this policy include but are not limited to:

a. Unwelcome sexual flirtations, advances, or propositions.
b. Verbal abuse of a sexual nature, including sexually derogatory remarks or graphic verbal comments about an individual's body.
c. Display in the workplace of sexually suggestive objects or pictures.
d. Sexually related or "off-color" jokes.
e. Making submission to or rejection of such conduct the basis for employment decisions.
f. Creating an intimidating, hostile, or offensive working environment by such conduct.

Any employee who believes that they have been the subject of sexual harassment should confidentially report the incident to their supervisor or me. Every reported incident of sexual harassment will be promptly investigated, and appropriate disciplinary action will be taken.

Everyone at the meeting knew the story as to why Mary Ann convened the meeting. There were no secrets at The Company. Everybody rolled their eyes and wondered why their precious time was being wasted. Approximately three months later, the aggrieved employee would be terminated for whatever reason they could come up with. No fuss no muss. Another chapter closed. And the beat goes on.

Nobody really questioned the policy. In many instances, the dismissed employee was probably happy to find employment elsewhere due to the constant embarrassment that hovered over them. The perpetrators, at best, got a slap on the wrist and, more often than not, associated the situation with having earned a badge of honor in the sense that it represented a conquest.

Mary Ann was embarrassed as she knew nobody except the aggrieved employees took these situations seriously. She knew it was wrong, but she had no choice but to do Daddy's bidding. In some instances, Daddy was caught between a rock and a hard place. Especially since Johnny Gumba was mowing through the ranks like Sherman tearing through the South. It was well-documented how Daddy and Johnny felt about one another. Daddy would have loved to run Gumba off, but he didn't want to risk shutting off the cash spigot. Johnny felt he was above reproach. These were his loan originators who were knocking it out of the park. He was the one pumping up the bottom line. He was responsible for the lavish lifestyles everybody enjoyed, including Daddy's. He took the same attitude that the fraternity in Animal House did in professing, "We may have taken a few liberties with these ladies," and then declaring it would be an affront to the United States of America to pursue the matter any further.

So, Mary Ann plodded along, followed the protocol, and wished that she could just one time bring these culprits to their knees. Given her choice, the prize catch would be Bugeater Chairman Eddie. She had come close on occasion only to be thwarted by the system and its unholy allegiance to the almighty buck. She was like the college basketball coach who labored for thirty years without getting a whiff of the final four and could only dream about it. And then, like a Godsend, her chance came flying out of the woodwork.

Once a year, the Bugeaters ventured over to the Chesapeake Bay to charter a boat and enjoy a day of rock fishing. This year, they went farther down the Bay than usual and decided to go a day early and stay overnight. They took out some rooms at a local motel, planning to get an early start on the fishing expedition. As at all Bugeater functions, alcohol consumption ruled the night, which turned into a drunk fest. Many unflattering photos were taken, which included the Clown Prince mooning the camera several times. They were, of course, severely hungover in the morning and late for the fishing boat. The captain was not pleased and perhaps deliberately trolled waters where there were no fish, which led to the Bugeaters coming home empty-handed. Wasn't the first time and wouldn't be the last.

When they resurfaced in the office, they shared stories and photographs with the staff. As always, a good laugh was had by all, as most employees were continuously amused by the Bugeaters' antics. They wished they could be as carefree and comical as this group of rogues.

Two days later, Linda, The Company's head underwriter, was working on one of the several loans she had on tap for the day. She finished the credit file and then moved on to the appraisal. She turned to the page where the photos of the comparables resided and broke out into a fit of hysterical laughter. There were three photos of very attractive homes beside one of a pimpled ass and a set of balls that would have made Seattle Slew proud. It was Bow mooning the camera on the fishing trip. The other underwriters rushed over and enjoyed a good laugh as well. Except for one. Wendy. Affectionately known as "The Detective" or The Company snitch. Devoid of a sense of humor, she grabbed the photos and rushed up to Mary Ann's office. She presented the evidence.

Mary Ann stood up beaming and exclaimed, "I think we finally got him." She then ran down to Eddie's office to confront him. Lucky for him, he was out playing golf. She would not be deterred. She waited until the evening and called him at home. "Be in my office at 8:00 a.m. sharp tomorrow morning," Mary Ann demanded.

Knowing full well what it was all about, Eddie said, "No problem. Will you be serving coffee?"

Disgusted, she slammed the phone down.

Next morning came, and Eddie was deliberately one-half hour late so he could irritate Mary Ann even more. He strolled into her office as she sat there glaring at him.

"Do you know why I summoned you here this morning?" she asked.

"Because you enjoy my company?" quipped Eddie.

Mary Ann slammed the photograph down on the desk. She shouted, "You are nothing but a purveyor of pornography."

He looked down at the photo and grinned. "But Mary Ann, you should know those aren't my balls."

Red-faced and shaking, she was speechless. All she could do was to point toward the doorway.

"Thanks for inviting me," he said, laughing. "Enjoy the rest of the day."

The result was very predictable. Both Daddy and Johnny Gumba had a good laugh when they heard about the incident. Eddie had skated once again. Mighty Mary Ann had struck out!

That summer, The Rolling Stones were coming to North America. It was the Voodoo Lounge Tour. Earl was a huge fan – this would be his tenth Stones concert. They were going to play two nights at RFK Stadium. Johnny Gumba arranged to get a bunch of tickets right near the stage. The Bugeaters were fired up!

The concert was on a Thursday night. To be in the proper frame of mind, the Bugeaters began to party at noontime, no one more so than

Tony B., Johnny Gumba's cousin. Tony had come to The Company one year ago at Gumba's behest. Nepotism at its finest. God bless him, but Tony knew less about loan origination after a year than when he showed up. Not to worry. Johnny put loans in Tony's name, had somebody else handle them, and then Tony got paid. You might say it was the quid pro quo for the fact that Gumba owned several acres of property in Culpeper, Virginia, where the marijuana crop needed overseeing. Tony was well-suited for that job and, therefore, didn't have a lot of time to devote to originating loans.

Tony was also a big Stones fan. He would travel to and from the stadium in Johnny's rented limo. He ingested as much booze and dope as a human being could on the way to, during, and on the way back. As always, The Stones put on a great show. When pressed later, Tony didn't have many details to offer up.

Amazingly enough, some concert-goers actually showed up at the office the next morning. Earl ran into Alicia B, who ran secondary marketing and was also Tony B's proud wife. She confirmed how messed up Tony got the night before and the fact that he probably wouldn't get out of bed the entire day. Earl knew an opportunity when he saw one, as he hated to see anyone sleep their life away.

Earl assembled the troops in the big conference room, including Tony's wife. Also present was a young staff member who could perfectly imitate the sing-song voice of a gentleman from Bombay, India. They put the phone on speaker box and called Tony's house. His son answered.

"Hello."

Indian voice. "I must speak with Mr. Tony immediately."

"Sorry. He's in bed sleeping."

"I am at his office. We have an appointment. I must speak to him now."

"Oh! Hang on. Let me see."

Five minutes later, Tony's tired voice came on the line. "Yo. What can I do for ya?"

"I am Patel Singh. Last evening, I left you a message on your pager that I would be at your office at 10:00 for a loan application. I say if you cannot be here to notify me. I hear nothing from you. I am here."

"Oh, wow, man. I didn't have my pager. I was at the Stones show. It was kick-ass, man. That dude Keith Richards can really riff it."

"I am not concerned with these matters. Who is the manager?"

"Calm down, brother. I'm gonna jump in the shower. I'll be there in a couple of minutes. I'll do ya loan for nuthin.'"

Everyone in the room cracked up. Then silence.

"Aw, shit. I'm going back to fuckin' bed," the befuddled Tony exclaimed.

Mary Ann didn't find out about that one. Not that it would have mattered. The Company cash register was ringing louder and more often than ever, with no end in sight.

As previously noted, what was considered harassment in the '80s and '90s would be radically different in modern times. Libby, the mother of Wendy, The Company snitch, was a loyal employee who had been with Daddy for many years. As loyal as she was, the one thing that always stuck in her craw was how the male loan originators got paid more on the builder loans that Daddy doled out than she did. When she finally mustered the courage to ask him about it, his response was, "You ain't got the right equipment."

One would be remiss if a certain type of reverse harassment was not noted.

Carol, one of the female Bugeaters, was a man in a woman's body. She could cuss like a sailor, drink like one, and copulate like one. One day, Reverend was in line for the computer where the loans were registered and locked in. As he stood waiting, someone came up behind him, grabbed his balls, and gave them a good squeeze. Reverend cried out and turned around. "Oh, it's you," he said. "I should have known. How was your weekend?"

Carol laughed and said, "Great. Fucked like a rabbit the whole time."

Then there was Nate, another female Bugeater. Nate was always enamored with Earl's physique and did not try to hide it. She frequently reminded him by loudly proclaiming, "I just wanna see you naked, Earl. I promise I won't touch! I just wanna look." She would yell from across the room, not caring who might have a client in their office. Some would tell her to keep it down, but that would only make her laugh. Amazingly, Nate never got in trouble for it. A casual observer may have recalled Clause B of the sexual harassment memo, which read "or graphic verbal comments about an individual's body." Fortunately for Nate, Earl had a good sense of humor and was not one to pursue a litigious solution.

Chapter 17

An Air of Flatulence

Since he was a young man, Eddie the Pec was always fascinated by his ability to pass gas at a moment's notice. Nothing was off limits – school, church, at home, and anywhere and everywhere. Many young men with similar tendencies eventually grew out of it. Not Eddie. If anything, he enjoyed it more over time. Many times, on the way to lunch with the Bugeaters or on the way back, he would rip one off and then put the windows in his SUV on auto lock. He would then yell, "lockdown," and laugh hysterically as all present gagged and suffered. Earl was continuously disgusted with Eddie's flatulence, but there was nothing he could do about it. When questioned, Eddie stated that it was simply a bodily function.

Eddie was well aware of the fact that Earl was less than pleased with his favorite pastime. He therefore made a point of farting every time he entered Earl's office. No one got more satisfaction out of this deviance than the Clown Prince himself. Bow recognized that Earl was the biggest thorn in his side and rejoiced in how he was under constant attack from Eddie. Bow decided to utilize all of his creative abilities when he hung a sign on Earl's office door that read "The Fart Room," Which became the official moniker for Earl's office, much to his consternation.

Around this same time frame, it was a very robust time for refinances. Interest rates near a historic low were responsible for the flurry of activity. Most of the Bugeaters were tonning it and making a very healthy living. Reverend was beginning to do well himself even though his average loan size was less than most of the loan originators at The Company due to how he covered a more rural area less affluent than Washington DC and its surrounding counties.

So, it was much to the delight of Reverend when a wealthy dentist was referred to him for a refinance, looking to borrow an amount three times the size of Reverend's average deal. If he was able to get it to closing, it would represent by far his largest commission ever. The problem was that even though the dentist was very well-heeled, he was a nickel-and-dimer. He would call every few days and inquire about that day's interest rate. He also consistently worked Reverend and tried to get him to lower the loan fees. Reverend was getting tired of it, but he really needed the big commission. He was also tired of the Bugeaters hovering around his desk, listening to him getting shopped by the dentist. He could not get him to commit, and he began to think the whole thing was pie in the sky.

And then it happened. The Bugeaters were coming back from another hearty L&N lunch. When they got off the elevator, Missy announced to Reverend that the dentist was on the phone, apparently wanting to lock in an interest rate. Reverend was, of course, happy, and so were the Bugeaters, who would get to watch him squirm once again.

They all rushed back to Reverend's office and circled his desk as he picked up the phone. Before he could say anything, a culprit stepped up and blew the vilest fart imaginable directly into the phone receiver.

The dentist on the line was stunned. "Isn't this a mortgage company?" he asked weakly.

Reverend couldn't help but laugh. "Let me get back to you on that."

Of course, he never did. One might ask why did he not report this outrage to Johnny Gumba? But he did. And what happened? Gumba laughed and blamed Reverend for letting the Bugeaters into his office. Easy come, easy go.

One of the great days in Eddie's adult life was the day he discovered the existence of the fart machine. The Casa Man, so named by his Hispanic client base, was a Company loan originator. He showed up one day with the device. Battery-operated, it made some of the most raucous sounds a human being could imagine. Eddie immediately drove to the mall in Tysons Corner to get one while they were still in stock. Once in his possession, he was like a kid on Christmas Day!

The next day, he brought it to the office and presented it to the Bugeaters. They were duly impressed. Earl knew Eddie would certainly get more than his money's worth from the machine. Eddie wanted to conduct a test on the machine, so he summoned Earl and Reverend, and they went outside to the front of the building. There was a flower pot adjacent to the front door. Eddie hid the machine amongst the flowers and turned it on. The Bugeaters positioned themselves twenty feet to the side of the pot. Then, they waited for some victims to appear.

Sure enough, five minutes later, two computer nerds came up the walkway toward the front door. When they reached the flower pot, Eddie hit the remote control and fired. "Wooooonk!" One of the nerds looked at the other and said, "Excuse me." The Bugeaters cracked up. They knew they had a winner.

Eddie used the machine on anybody any time he could. For example, Earl's wife would bring their young children to the office on occasion. Eddie would terrorize their son with the machine, such that for years, any time Eddie called Earl at home in the evening, his son would ask, "Is that the guy with the fart machine?"

As much as the Bugeaters liked to lunch at L&N, they would deviate once in a while. There was a very good Italian restaurant in a nearby shopping plaza they also favored. Eddie knew the owner, Mike, who loved to wager on NFL games. Eddie was more than happy to help him with that endeavor as he would get paid when Mike lost, which was basically every weekend.

The restaurant had outdoor seating with flower pots flanking the tables. The tables were lined up adjacent to the sidewalk. Eddie determined that it represented a potentially great set-up for the fart machine. The Bugeaters selected a table, and Eddie positioned the machine three flower pots away.

Fortunately, there was a lot of sidewalk traffic that day. Eddie fired off the machine several times with varying degrees of success. Some people scowled, and some people laughed. Some didn't react at all, as they apparently did not wish to take the bait. But there was no question they heard it. With a fresh battery in tow, the machine was a loud force to be reckoned with.

Then, along came a good-looking sixty-year-old woman heading into the restaurant. Eddie fired as she opened the front door. She turned around and burst out laughing. "Where can I get one of those?" she asked.

Unbeknownst to the Bugeaters, Mike, the owner, had watched these events unfold. He rushed over and plucked the fart machine out of the flower pot. He walked down the sidewalk to the nearest trash can and deposited the machine. Mike returned, and as he entered the restaurant, he cried, "Enough!"

The Bugeaters didn't know what to do. As they sat there looking sheepish, the lady walked down to the trash can and retrieved the machine. She brought it to the Bugeaters' table and put it down. She was laughing. "I love it, boys. Keep it up."

The Bugeaters took her words to heart and vowed to do so.

As previously noted, loan originators in general and certainly the Bugeaters, were a very competitive group. At every loan officer meeting, they revealed company and individual production numbers.

Everybody knew who was doing business and who wasn't. If you weren't doing business and the Bugeaters liked you, they would leave you alone. If you were Ab La Sword, they would torture you. There was clearly a pecking order based on loan production.

There was also a supposed pecking order based on famous customer relationships. Eddie made it his business to know every famous person he could and then let everybody else know about it. See Mike Wilbon. To his credit, he was able to parlay many such relationships into the mortgage banking business.

One such group was the Washington Redskins. Eddie had established a relationship with a young assistant who eventually became the team's general manager, which led to Eddie being the team's preferred lender whenever one of the players wanted to buy a house. He was able to close many transactions for the players of the professional sports team, which was far and away the most popular in the metropolitan Washington, DC, area. And he wasn't shy about letting anybody know all about it who would listen.

So, of course, when Eddie set up a loan application with a Redskin linebacker, he announced it to the entire Company. Although used to it, the rank and file, were also tired of it. None more so than Charli, Eddie's processor. She had to tolerate him for eight hours a day, which would test the mettle of any strong-minded individual. When she heard the Redskin was coming in tomorrow, she hatched a plan.

Eddie strutted in at 10:00 a.m., as usual. He was dressed to the nines, as he always thought he would impress his famous clientele. He had an announcement for all Company personnel.

"You all know who I'm meeting with this morning. Remember, I don't ask your clients for their autographs. Don't you dare ask mine."

An Air of Flatulence

Charli, whose desk was outside Eddie's office, was on high alert. When Eddie went to the men's room five minutes before the Redskin was due to arrive, she sprang into action. She entered his office and retrieved the fart machine from the top drawer. She turned it on, placed it on the floor under the guest chair, and confiscated the remote control. Then, Charli went out to the hallway and assembled a number of the troops who knew what was going on. They were loving this.

Upon his client's arrival, Eddie greeted him in the lobby so he could walk him back and be seen by everybody. They entered his office.

"Have a seat, Greg. Let's get this application started. What is your current address?"

As Greg began to answer, Charli pulled the trigger. "Wooooonk."

Both men turned red.

"Greg. Do you have to use the men's room?"

"I was about to ask you the same question."

Eddie looked down and saw the machine. He grabbed it and flung it out into the hallway. "Looks like we've got a bunch of pranksters around here."

Charli and the crew busted a gut laughing. At that moment, all of the aggravation was forgotten.

Most of the other Bugeaters were not really concerned about originating loans from celebrity clients. To them, a loan was a loan, and they all paid the same. However, B.B. was new to The Company and the Bugeaters, and he was looking to make his bones. So, it was his extreme pleasure to announce to the Bugeaters that, in the following week, a Dutch countess was coming in for a loan application.

Of course, the subject of conversation for the next week at lunch was the Countess. None of the Bugeaters had seen a real Countess, let alone originated a loan for one. B.B. was enjoying the newfound attention. Speculation was rampant. What was she on a scale of one to ten? What kind of expensive clothes and jewelry would she have on when she came in? How did one converse with a Countess? These questions would all be answered next Tuesday morning.

Earl had alerted Missy to let the Bugeaters know when the Countess arrived. Earl got the call, and the Bugeaters assembled in the office next door to B.B.'s office. Two minutes later, down the hall came B.B. with his new client. His face was fire-engine red, and he looked like he had just swallowed a canary. The Countess was a tad overweight and wore a frumpy black dress with no jewelry. She had more hair under her arms and on her legs than some of the Bugeaters had on their heads. B.B. brought her into his office and was going to attempt to conduct business.

The Bugeaters assumed their customary position just outside B.B.'s door. As he began to ask the standard loan application questions, the good Countess raised her right leg and passed gas. It was most audible out in the hallway. She laughed and continued on. B.B. wanted to crawl into a hole. The Bugeaters were laughing so hard they could no longer stay outside B.B.'s door.

They were extremely gratified that they had been finally exposed to true royalty.

Then there was the time the Bugeaters attended a meeting of loan originators affiliated with The Company. Approximately two hundred people assembled in a very large conference hall. The participants had taken a break and were now seated, waiting for the proceedings to begin once again. All of a sudden, Eddie hit Earl in the shoulder and said, "Look at this." A middle-aged gentleman was leaning back in his chair with a cigarette lighter pointed at his crotch. A stream of fire shot out, resembling an expulsion from a rocket ship. The good news was the meeting started up, so he couldn't continue lighting his gas. The bad news was he was one of the managers.

Chapter 18

Saturday Night Live Mortgage

As previously noted, Earl grew up in Boston, Massachusetts. One thing ingrained in Boston culture is that everyone has a nickname. To this day, Earl cannot recall any of his friends who went by their given name. Some people even had more than one. When Earl moved down to the DC area in 1979, he carried on the tradition of creating nicknames for his friends and associates. Certainly, all of the Bugeaters had nicknames. Earl was responsible for many of them. But even he had never worked for a company that had a nickname. Reverend got the credit for this. After a certain incident, which, of course, involved Eddie the Pec (amongst other things), he emphatically stated, "This place is Saturday Night Live Mortgage."

In those days, it was customary that when a loan originator went on vacation, a colleague would "cover their pager." In addition to fielding all pager and phone calls, that individual would handle anything relating to the vacationer's business. As all originators were on one hundred percent commission, one could not afford to shut off the spigot for two reasons. One, there would be no income, which, given the way these guys lived, was not plausible. Second, realtors would take their business elsewhere the moment they could not reach someone. See the Realtors (or, Pigeons in the Park?) chapter.

When it came to determining who would cover whose pager, Earl drew the short straw. He got Eddie. When things got too crazy, he rationalized that he could have drawn the Clown Prince. Probably six of one or half dozen of another.

So, when Eddie announced that he would be traveling to Colorado for a week of mountain fishing and dope-smoking, Earl began his mental preparation. It was like preparing for a prize fight or a seventh game. You tried to remain confident, but sometimes the nerves took over. This was one of those times. Earl had a bad feeling about this one. His premonition would be confirmed three times over.

Amazingly, Monday went by without a hitch. Tuesday morning came around, and Earl was very busy trying to take care of his own business. It was a very busy time, and it took ten hours per day to keep up. Earl was running from one thing to the next when his phone rang.

"Hello, this is Earl."

"This is Sally Smith. I was told to call you. Eddie is refinancing our property, or at least I think he is. The appraiser is here at our home right now, and there seems to be a misunderstanding."

Earl's first thought was, *here we go again.* "A misunderstanding? And what might that be, Mrs. Smith?"

"We are trying to pay off our existing mortgage and get as much cash back as possible. Sometime in the future, we are going to perform some extensive renovations to our home. We're not entirely sure what we are going to do, but we have some good ideas. Eddie said to tell the appraiser when he came out what we think we want to do so he will give that much more value to the appraisal. I mentioned this to the appraiser, and he is looking at me like I have eight heads."

Earl was about to say he should be, but he thought better of it. "Perhaps Eddie knows of some creative financing that the appraiser and I are not aware of. I will be sure to have him take it up with you when he gets back."

"Well, we need to get this thing moving. Then send me a Good-Faith Estimate."

"Mrs. Smith, please refer to the one Eddie provided to you."

"He did not provide one."

"He must have."

"He did not, and I want you to send one today."

Earl was starting to lose it. If he sent an estimate with accurate figures, the bottom line would undoubtedly be substantially higher than some BS verbal numbers Eddie threw out there in the interest of getting the deal. Earl was not going to fall into that trap. "I promise I will ask him to send you one as soon as he gets back. Thanks for calling. Have a nice day."

Earl hung up and waited for the next shoe to drop. The phone rang ten minutes later.

"Hello, this is Earl."

"What the hell is he doing now?"

"Tom?"

The appraiser was not happy. "I don't know how the hell you deal with this crap. You're a better man than I. Tell that yo-yo to call me when he gets back."

Earl's sixth sense had kicked in. It was going to be a long, long week. The phone rang again.

"Hello, this is Earl."

"Hi. This is Bob Goldberg. Eddie told me to call you. I want to get my loan locked in as we're getting close to closing."

"Sure, Mr. Goldberg. What program are you interested in?"

"The 7-23."

"Okay. Let me pull up today's rates."

Earl disclosed the current rate. Mr. Goldberg accepted the terms and seemed exceptionally pleased. Earl said he would get it locked in as soon as they got off the phone. As they hung up, Earl thought to himself, *that was almost too easy.*

Thirty minutes later, Daddy stormed into Earl's office and slammed the door shut. "What the hell is going on around here?" he demanded.

Earl was stunned. "I'm sorry. What do you mean?"

"What's going on with this guy, Goldberg?"

"I'm covering Eddie's pager. Goldberg called and asked me to lock his loan in, so I did."

"Great. The only problem with that is Goldberg's already locked in. I'm going to get to the bottom of this. I'll get back to you."

For the next hour, Earl tried to get caught up on his phone calls.

Then Daddy resurfaced. "Goldberg and his wife are going to be here at 10:00 a.m. next Tuesday morning. I want you at this meeting."

Earl tried to hide his glee. "I'll be there."

"Good," said Daddy as he strutted out.

As stressed out as he was, Earl was ecstatic. He would get to personally witness the dressing down of Eddie. Tuesday morning couldn't come soon enough.

Earl went back to his own business. Mid-afternoon came around, and he was actually making some headway. Then the shoe dropped again. Charli, Eddie's processor, poked her head into Earl's office and asked if he had a minute. Earl realized he had just hit the trifecta.

"Earl, do you know anything about the Jackson loan?" Charli asked.

Wearily, Earl responded, "No. Should I?"

"Mr. Jackson just called. He wanted to know if his loan is approved because he is closing on Friday. He said he has to close on Friday as his loan balloons then."

"And?"

"I don't have a Jackson file."

"Say what?"

"I never knew this loan existed until he just called."

Earl was beside himself. "Come on. Let's check his office."

They walked down the hall to Eddie's office. They encountered ten manila folders sitting on the top of his credenza. Earl began to sift through the folders and came upon one marked "Jackson." He opened it and reviewed the loan application. He then let out a loud groan.

"What's the matter?" asked Charli.

"We can't do this loan. Jackson owns seven properties. Try to get a hold of Eddie and find out what the hell he is thinking."

(Note: Guidelines at the time precluded The Company from lending to anybody who owned more than one principal residence and three investment properties.)

Charli got back to Earl the next day. "I got a hold of him. He told me the loan doesn't balloon until next month. I told him no, it comes due this Friday. He said, 'Oh well, I'll deal with it next week.' Personally, I think he was smoking a bone while we were talking."

"I'm not surprised," said Earl. "I'm sure he'll come up with a great solution."

(The great solution was that Earl referred Jackson to a subprime lender who charged him fourteen percent and paid Eddie a robust referral fee.)

Somehow, Earl survived the rest of the week in one piece. He was actually able to get caught up on his own business and, by working with Charli, fend off any other problems pertaining to Eddie. Earl maintained the utmost level of respect for Charli as she was cursed by also having to process for the Clown Prince and Reverend. As previously noted, she was duly honored with the lifetime Joan of Arc award by The Bugeater Lunch and Supper Club.

Five o'clock Friday afternoon came around, and Earl breathed a huge sigh of relief. He was off the clock. He would spend the weekend salivating at the prospect of Eddie being called on the carpet next Tuesday morning.

Earl rolled in early Monday morning and eagerly waited for Eddie to post up. Eddie strolled in at 10:30 and proceeded to regale the staff with tales of his fishing exploits. Earl referenced the fact that the Goldbergs were coming in tomorrow, and how worried was he? Eddie totally pooh-poohed it, noting that, as always, he had done nothing wrong. Earl surmised to himself that he would be singing a different tune tomorrow.

Tuesday morning came around, and the Bugeaters were both excited and jealous because Earl alone would be witness to the evisceration of Eddie. Earl arrived at the big conference room at 10:00 sharp.

Daddy and the Goldbergs were already present. The Goldbergs were dressed like they were going to a Jimmy Buffet concert. Tank tops, Bermuda shorts, sandals, and lots of gold jewelry to boot. Daddy, in his three-piece suit and severe hangover mode, introduced the disgruntled clients. Eddie arrived five minutes late. Daddy, feeling like death warmed over, was not pleased. He motioned to Eddie to sit down across the conference table. Eddie's forehead was the color of a newly polished fire engine.

Earl stared at the floor, as it was all he could do to refrain from bursting out in laughter.

Daddy called the meeting to order. "Thank you, folks, for traveling this great distance to be here today. Mr. Goldberg, will you be kind enough to relate to us what has transpired over the course of this transaction?"

"Thank you for meeting with us and trying to resolve this situation," said Mr. Goldberg. "I was shopping around for loan rates to refinance our rental condo in Georgetown, and a friend mentioned that I should call The Company. So, I called in, and the receptionist transferred me to Eddie here. I explained our situation and asked that he quote us a rate. He said he would get back to me. He called back later that day and quoted a rate significantly lower than the other quotes we had received. So, I said we would do the loan with him."

"And then what happened?" asked Daddy.

"He sent us a loan package with an application. We filled out the information and sent it back with the required documentation, such as our tax returns. He called and asked me to follow up with him at such time that I wanted to lock in the rate."

"You mentioned that when you first called in, you told him you rent the property?"

"Yes. We've owned the property for five years. It's always been an investment property."

All of a sudden, the lightbulb went on for Earl. He realized what had happened. In his zeal to land Goldberg's business, Eddie had quoted him a rate for a second home, which is significantly lower than the rates for a rental property. He had mentioned Goldberg might call in and that he was refinancing a second home. He forgot that Schedule E of the tax returns would show rental income, which would automatically qualify it as an investment property. Earl looked over at Daddy and noticed the steam pouring out of him.

"So, you called to lock in?"

"Yes. On the fifth. I was told that Eddie was out of town, so I was transferred to his assistant, Earl."

Earl couldn't contain himself. "I am not his assistant."

Daddy exclaimed, "That's right. He's not his assistant."

"Okay. Got it," said Goldberg. "In any event, Earl said he would lock us into a rate that was most favorable. Then, I get a financing agreement faxed to us from the processor that shows a significantly higher rate. I called her and said, 'This must be a mistake.' She said, 'There is no mistake. This is the correct rate.' Then I got a call from you asking me why I tried to lock in twice. I am simply trying to refinance this property. Frankly, this whole thing has been like Saturday Night Live."

Anybody familiar with Daddy knew he was a proud man. He had built The Company from scratch into the most successful mortgage banking operation in the DC metropolitan area. That he was forced, with a pounding head, to listen to a customer put forth a less than favorable "who struck John" scenario and cap it off with reference to a comedy show did not bode well for Eddie.

"Earl," barked Daddy. "Thank you for your time. You can go about your business."

Earl and Eddie stood up and headed for the door.

Daddy motioned to Eddie. "Have a seat. We're not done."

Earl left the room, knowing what he would miss.

Daddy proceeded to berate and humiliate Eddie. He apologized profusely to the Goldbergs and assured them that this was an aberration, that neither he nor The Company did business in this manner. He stripped Eddie of his full commission and used it in part to make the Goldbergs whole for having to swallow a rate that was not properly disclosed to them. The Goldbergs thanked Daddy and assured him that there were no hard feelings. Eddie put his tail between his legs yet again and retreated to his office where the Bugeaters awaited. They pounced on him unmercifully. Eddie, of course, blamed everybody but himself. The more things changed, the more they stayed the same.

While Mr. Goldberg likened his mortgage experience to having dealt with a Saturday-Night-Live-like character, this was not Eddie's first rodeo in show business. He had befriended a group of Pakistanis who hung around a gas station where Eddie lived in Falls Church. He stopped by for a fill-up one day when one of the Pakistani gentlemen approached him and announced they were working on producing a blockbuster movie. It was entitled *White Gold* (see the attached advertisement) and had the potential to be one of the epic productions of that generation. Eddie's antenna went up. He was offered the role of a heroin smuggler arrested by the authorities. Due to budget constraints, Eddie would not be compensated for his efforts, but they did offer lunch on the day of filming. The gas station served as headquarters for the production, which was in Pakistani and dubbed in English.

The film was actually released. Apparently, it did better in Pakistan than in the USA. Nobody was getting rich, as evidenced by the fact that the producers remained in the gas station business. As for Eddie, although his fame was fleeting, it did bear some fruit. He was riding in a DC taxi cab some years later, driven by a Pakistani man. The cabbie mentioned that Eddie looked familiar. At first, Eddie was puzzled, but then he smiled.

"White Gold," exclaimed Eddie. "Yes."

"Yes. The best!" cried the cabbie.

Eddie, a man of many self-proclaimed talents, was now a bona fide movie star.

SARFRAZ TARIQ PRESENTS
ZAFAR ART PRODUCTION
"WHITE GOLD" GEVA COLOR

Produced & Direced by
ZAFAR SHABAB

Associate Producers
SARFRAZ TARIQ (U.S.A.) - NASEEM ZAFAR SHABAB (Pak) - NAEEM ZAFAR SHABAB (Pak)

Written by : **BASHIR NIAZ**   Music : **M. ASHRAF**   Cinematography : **IMTIAZ QURESHI (CAP)**
Lyrics : **KHWAJA PERVEZ**   Editing : **TAHIR RIAZ**   Associate Director : **ASHRAF ALI CHACHA**

Staring : **VAGIRA, NOOR NAGHMI, PENNY PERNA, KEVIN OMERA, MARIAN GAFI ALI SHOAB, HASAN ZEDI, AISHA KHAN, MUNIR AHMAD, DAVID SIMON, JIM ANDERSON IBRAHIM, MIKE CACEDI, GEORG, FARAH, ARIF DAR, NANNA & MOHAMMAD ALI.**

Singers : **A. NAYYAR, SHAUKAT ALI, MEHNAZ, RAJAB ALI, NAHEED AKHTAR & MUSARAT NAZIR**

Art Director	Production	Processed at	Fights
LATEEF	MOHD IQBAL (Pak)	INTERNATIONAL	QAISAR MASTANA
Dresses	JOHN (USA)	STUDIOS KARACHI	Chief Asstt. Director
MARSHAL (USA)	Dubbing	Accounts	NAEEM SHEHZAD
GAMNI TAILORS	REHANA, AURANGZEB	BARKAT ALI	Chief Asstt. Photography
(Sri Lanka)	ALI AHMA,D, IRSA	Processing	EJAZ QURESHI
FITWELL TAILORS (Pak)	SHAFIA BILLA	AMIR ALI, ANWAR	Completed at
Make up	Song Recording	Stills	UNITED STATES OF.
NASIR KHAN (Pak)	SOHAIL NAGMI	MIRZA MUNIR BAIG	AMERICA
LORD (USA)	Dialogue Recording	Publicity	Electrician
Hair Style	GULZAR ALI	M: AFZAL STUDIO	IBRAHIM
LILY (USA)	Re-Recording	S. IQBAL	Traveling Agent
	M. ZAFAR	Publicity Manager	ALI TALIA
		M. YOUNUS BUTT	

ASSISTANTS

Direction : ROBERT	Stills : MUKHTAR BUTT, ASLAM	Cinematography : LATIF ALI JAN
Electric : KUCHA, LIAQUAT	Sound : M. ZAFAR	Music : M. ARSHAD
Recording : MOHAMMAD ATTA	Make up : ROZY	Editing : HASAN ALI, FIDA
Production : STENLAY, SAJJAD	Dress Master : T. N. GARNER	

"White Gold"

Gold and Silver are those two metals which were evaluated the first of all in this world.

When one has the madness of collecting gold, one becomes Midas. Concerning his desire for gold, there is a famous story about him. He prayed to God that he may be given the power to touch anything and turn it into gold. He was given that power.

He touched his bed and it turned into solio gold : he cried with joy. He touched a table and it became a table of gold : he was mad with joy. To share this joy with his queen, he took her into his arms. Lo ! The queen at once turned into a golden statue. He became very sad. Food was placed before him and as he put a hot potato into his mouth, it became a hot piece of gold and burnt his tongue. He prayed that that power may be taken from him. His prayer was granted.

In our story, that fellow lived in America and led the life of Lords. He was termed the King of "White Gold". Previously in history, it was Midas of Gold ; today in America, he was the Midas of heroin.. When that gold bit him and his body burst with poison, he gave a message. This message is worth seeing on the screen as well as is a thing which should serve as a lesson to the world.

وائٹ گولڈ ۔ سونا اور چاندی وہ دو دھاتیں ہیں جن کی اس دنیا میں سب سے پہلے قیمت مقرر ہوئی ۔

سنیما کے کاہن ہو تو آدمی کو خود قارون بنا دے ۔ سونے کے حوالے سے ایک بادشاہ کا قصّہ بہت مشہور ہے ۔ بھی سے خدا سے دعا مانگی تھی ۔ مجھے یہ طاقت دے کہ میں جس چیز کو ہاتھ لگاؤں وہ سونا ہو جائے ۔ اس کی دعا قبول ہوئی ۔ اس نے پلنگ کو ہاتھ لگایا وہ سونے کا ہوگیا ۔ وہ خوشی سے پاگل ہو گیا ۔ اس نے میز کو ہاتھ لگایا وہ سونے کی ہوگئی ۔ وہ اپنی ملکہ سے جا لپٹا وہ بھی سونے کی مجسمہ بن گئی ۔ وہ نڈھال ہوا ۔ اس کے سامنے کھانا کیا جیسے اس نے گرم آلو اٹھا کر منہ میں رکھا تو سونے کا گرم ٹکڑا ہو کر اس کی زبان جل گئی اس نے کہا ۔ نہیں مجھے سونا نہیں چاہیے ۔ بھاری کھانی میں ۔ وہ شخص امریکہ میں رہتا تھا ۔ لارڈز کی طرح جیتا ۔ آج کے بدترین نشے کو وائٹ گولڈ کہتا ہے اور خود کنگ آف وائٹ گولڈ کہلاتا ۔ کل تاریخ میں سونے کا قارون تھا ۔ آج امریکہ میں سونے کا ہیروئن کا قارون ہے ۔ سونے نے جب اسے ڈسا زہر اس کے کاسہ سر پھٹا ۔ تو اس نے ایسا پیغام دیا وہ دیکھنے کی چیز بھی ہے ۔ دنیا کے لیے عبرت حاصل کرنے کی چیز بھی بھلا ئے ۔

Chapter 19

Mortgage Banker of the Year

The basis of the Bugeater Lunch and Supper Club was electing the winner of the Mortgage Banker of the Year award. Earl, the Club Secretary, would document all the crazy screwball antics throughout the year. Then, at the end of each year, a date in December would be selected for election day. The day's agenda was well-established and always included heavy drinking, shooting pool, and visiting a strip club. The day ended with a dinner where they would vote on the Mortgage Banker of the Year award winner and other awards.

Once the date was set, it was greatly anticipated by club members. One particular year, they made the mistake of allowing Eddie the Pec to set the agenda for the dinner and the strip club. Early in the day, the group shot pool and had lunch. Eddie informed the Bugeaters that he'd done loans for this guy who has a place in DC called Louie's Rogue, and he had agreed to host the evening's festivities. Eddie added that, as a special bonus, the chef is going to stay late that night and make them a special meal.

The first warning sign was that they had to go through a metal detector to get into the place. The second warning was, as crazy as it sounds, there was a pregnant stripper. A very pregnant stripper.

Louie's Rogue was the Saturday Night Live of strip clubs. The Bugeaters had never seen anything like this before. The special dinner that the chef was supposed to stay and prepare consisted of a can of Chef Boyardee Spaghetti-Os heated by a stern-o can. In his drunken stupor, Bow the Clown Prince wolfed down the can's contents, the only food available. Even by Eddie's standards, that was off the rails.

Then, it got worse. Earl's pager went off (remember, this was in the days before cell phones), and he could see a row of pay phones above all the pool tables. He went up there to call the pager to see who the hell was looking for him. A drunkard was standing ten feet away from Earl, urinating on the floor. The one lady present, Nate, who Earl called Nathan, witnessed this ugly scene and broke down crying. That was the last straw; they were out of there. When confronted on this disastrous evening, Eddie just said, "I was just screwing with you guys."

It's worth mentioning, although not tied to the Bugeaters, another major event that happened every December. The Mortgage Bankers Association hosted the Wine and Cheese party. It was a black-tie industry party for mortgage bankers in a rented hotel ballroom. Everybody got dressed up. There was more cocaine in that room than in Johnny Depp's movie *Blow*. Many of these loan originators had major league egos and some of them would bring their W-2s to show people how much money they made the year before.

One year, Eddie and Earl went to this party, and when they were at the office the next morning, they heard the rumor that Johnny Gumba was shacked up at the hotel with one of the processors. So, of course, they called the hotel and had the front desk patch them through to Johnny's room; the processor answered the phone. From Gumba's perspective, it was another notch in his belt. Still, the antic left The Company wide open to another sexual harassment situation, which was well documented in The Company – A Human Resources Nightmare chapter.

Getting back to the Mortgage Banker of the Year awards, Earl was kept busy documenting the wealth of stories accumulated throughout the years. An award winner could potentially have cumulative stories. For example, a contestant could have garnered some points toward the award in 1991, and then their actions in 1992 could put them across the finish line for a win. Some of these stories are covered in previous chapters, however, they're referenced again because of what contributed to those contestants winning the award or being in contention for it.

Reverend won the award in 1992 and actually hung the plaque in his office. Customers would come in and say, "Oh, you must be a big shot because you won this award." Reverend would say he wanted to be humble about these things, but his customers thought it was a legitimate award and for something he'd want to be proud of. They probably didn't read the inscription that identified the Bugeater Lunch and Supper Club and only focused on his name and the picture of the businessman holding a briefcase on the plaque. They thought, wow, this guy must be something special.

As all award winners and contestants tended to have multiple stories that contributed to their recognition, the same was true for Reverend. This first story about Reverend hasn't been mentioned before, fondly referred to as "the call from the mall." Reverend was financing a home out in the boondocks, west of Fairfax County, a much more rural area. This gentleman's house was up in the hills where the houses are on well and septic rather than city water and sewer. It should be noted that when a house is on well and septic, the systems have to be inspected and receive a clean rating because no lender wants to lend money on a house with a septic system that's gone bad. In this case, it was the last piece of the puzzle to get the loan closed.

Because the loan was due to close the next day, Reverend told the closing manager that he would accompany the inspector to the home so he could call from the property and let her know the inspection passed. They didn't have time to wait for the certificate to be delivered, as was the norm. The closing manager agreed to Reverend's request to close with a phone call and follow up with the certificate on Monday.

Instead of driving to the home to meet the inspector, Reverend goes one mile to the Fair Oaks Mall. Reverend, who spent most of his time in bowling alleys and golf courses, didn't want to spend his valuable time driving to the boondocks to meet an inspector. He finds a payphone at the mall and calls the manager, and, as he's explaining that everything's going fine with the inspection, all of a sudden, a voice comes over the loudspeaker in the mall and loudly says, "There will be a Sears tire sale for Firestone and Dunlop products at two o'clock today at twenty percent off."

The manager heard the broadcast and said, "What's that?"

Reverend says, "Oh, I have my car radio on."

She accepted that explanation, and they went ahead and closed the loan. The inspection failed, adding further intrigue to the story. After the smoke cleared, he was asked, "Why would you do that?" As Earl always said, the answer was, "Follow the money." Closing the loan that day would bump Reverend's commission to a higher level for all loans that were closed that month.

Eventually, they resolved the situation after bringing the septic system to a passing grade. However, this was not your classic "all's well that ends well." The manager made it perfectly clear Reverend could never expect another favor from her. From the Bugeaters' perspective, as great as the entire story was, the fact that increased profit was Reverend's motivation was the most impressive aspect to them.

The second Reverend story is about Hector, who drove three hours to do a refinance and, of course, Reverend didn't feel it necessary to show up because he was having lunch with Bow over at L&N Seafood. Refer to Chapter 13, An Equal Opportunity Membership, for the full story. Here are a few questions one might reasonably ask:

Who blows off a meeting with a loan applicant who had to drive three hours to get there? Just to go to lunch with the same guy you had lunch with at the same place for the past three days? And what did Reverend promise this gentleman to get him to drive three hours? Why would Reverend believe that this gentleman, who had driven three hours to get to The Company, where he was unceremoniously blown off, and had to drive three hours back to Salisbury, MD, would then present himself at the office at 9 a.m. the next morning to confront Reverend? Finally, when Reverend was summoned by Missy, the receptionist, to the lobby to greet the "fictitious" Hector, how did he mistake Mr. Bob Smith for Hector, who is Hispanic? Perhaps you could answer some or all of these questions, but the Bugeaters certainly could not.

Then there is the one about Reverend and Mrs. Chen. For the full story, refer to Chapter 11, Loan Applicants or Victims? The beauty of the Mrs. Chen story was that Earl just happened to be standing there to overhear Reverend's response to the problem, "Mrs. Chen, I really wish it could be one." Earl thought, "Oh, my God. Are you joking? Did you just say what I think you said?" Then, Johnny Gumba got a hold of it and jacked the price up, and the rest is duly noted. This story begs the question how many things happened that Earl or another Bugeater wasn't present to witness and record for this book? Inasmuch as these 19 chapters portray many antics, how many more could have been written if every misdeed was known?

Then there was Reverend's call with the dentist, maybe the funniest thing that Earl saw the entire time because it was spontaneous. Refer to Chapter 17, An Air of Flatulence, for the full story. The dentist had been working Reverend over for weeks to get lower fees and a lower rate, and the Bugeaters were well informed about the situation. When they all came back from lunch one day and heard Missy tell Reverend, "The Dentist is on the phone," the Bugeaters were visibly excited and all marched in line behind him to his office. The prevailing thought was they would be able to hear The Dentist work Reverend over again, but The Culprit had another idea and sprung into action. The combination of the flatulence, the laughter, and the element of surprise almost rendered the dentist speechless.

Like most other people, the well-to-do dentist, who had never experienced such a situation, could only ask, "Isn't this a mortgage company?" Had he been a lawyer, he would have known never to ask a question you don't know the answer to. When he went home that night, his wife asked if he got their loan locked in. He explained what happened. She asked, "Isn't it a mortgage company?"

It was somewhat amazing that Reverend lost the biggest commission he would have ever earned, and The Company lost sizeable revenue, as well. Yet, everyone involved, including Johnny Gumba, thought the situation was hysterically funny. And the beauty of the whole story is that Johnny Gumba blamed Reverend for it because he said, "You let those guys in your office. You shouldn't have done that."

Then, there's Eddie the Pec. The Bugeaters had a laundry list of stories on him. When Earl first came to The Company, he knew Eddie a bit, but not really well. Earl was trying to get acclimated to the loan programs and learn about The Company as a whole. In those days, every lender The Company sold loans to had their own manual of rules and regulations. They were the size of phone books. There was a bank out of Cleveland called Cardinal Bank, and The Company was selling them a lot of arms (adjustable-rate mortgages). A three, five, or seven-year arm is fixed for the first three, five, or seven years and then becomes an adjustable rate. The Washington Post real estate section would write about a variety of mortgage loan programs that would often become a flavor of the day for mortgage customers. For example, they would write an article listing the benefits of a 15-year mortgage, resulting in many customers asking for 15-year loans.

The flavor of the day at this time was the convertibility of arms, which meant that some of these adjustable rates had an option to convert to a fixed rate after the initial three, five, or seven-year term – an attractive feature to customers.

So, Earl is reading through all this material, and Eddie comes walking past his office and says hello. Earl says, "Hey, Eddie, I'm brushing up on these Cardinal arms here. Are they convertible?"

Eddie looks at Earl like he has eight heads, and he says, "Hell, I don't know. I tell them they are." And then he just keeps walking.

Earl thought to himself, "Okay, welcome to The Company."

There is the duly noted Goldberg story involving Eddie, which led to the name of Chapter 18, Saturday Night Live Mortgage. Earl was having a rough week covering Eddie's pager. But he was rewarded when Daddy requested Earl to attend his meeting with the Goldbergs. One would have to be a member of the Bugeater group to appreciate the significance of this opportunity. The degree of envy and jealousy the Bugeaters had for Earl was off the charts, as he would be the only one to witness Eddie being eviscerated by Daddy. It was maybe the greatest day of Earl's life in the mortgage business. The visual of this meeting has stayed with Earl forever.

At that meeting, Daddy was hung over, eyes burning, working on three hours of sleep. Eddie's face was the color of a fire engine. And a Jimmy Buffet look-alike telling Daddy, who was very proud of the business he had built, that in essence, The Company was a freakin' joke, like Saturday Night Live Mortgage. One would have to have been present in that room to appreciate the level of tension that existed. The coup de grâce of the meeting was when Daddy dismissed Earl, and, as Eddie tried to follow Earl out of the room, Daddy commanded him back to his seat. It was time for Eddie to pay the piper.

Another great story involved a different character named Eddie. They called him Eddie D. He had left The Company and went to work for a competitor.

Earl was at the office one afternoon, and Eddie the Pec comes rolling in, and he's fired up. Earl says, "So now what's the matter?"

Eddie says, "Goddamnit. I was down at the Prudential office this afternoon. You know who was in there? Eddie D was in there. What the hell is he doing in my office?"

Each loan officer had territories with individual real estate offices assigned to them.

Earl said, "Eddie, the guy's a competitor now. What do you think he's gonna do? He's soliciting business."

"Well, shit, that's my office. I've had enough of this," Eddie said.

Right then, the light bulb went on for Earl. Earl went to see Charli. He knew there was a guy in that office that Eddie did a lot of business with. Earl asked Charli to get him a contract from this realtor, Jake. She finds a contract from one of Jake's transactions. Earl made a copy and whited out everything.

It's important to note that, at that time, the average loan size was in the $200,000 range. So, Earl changes the contract to reflect a sale price of $875,000 and a $700,000 loan. He fills in all the other information and writes up a fax cover sheet that reads, "Dear Eddie,

Thanks for all your great work. Here's a real nice one for you." Then, they sent the fake contract and the cover sheet to the fax machine where everybody received their faxes. All the Bugeaters were in on this one. Next, Earl says to Nate, "Nate, when this comes through the fax, retrieve it and give it to Eddie."

And then they all went down to Johnny Gumba's office to sit there because they knew what was coming. Sure enough, Eddie got it and, thinking the fax was meant for Eddie D., but sent to the wrong fax number, comes flying down the hall, and charges into Gumba's office, visibly upset, where the Bugeaters are assembled.

Gumba asks Eddie, "What's wrong?"

"Check out this son of a bitch, Jake. I've been doing this guy's shitty FHA loans for ten years. And look at this. Look at this!"

"Eddie, what is it?" everyone asks.

"Well, it's a deal for Eddie D, and Jake sent it to the wrong fax machine."

Earl said, "Oh, my God. That's terrible. This is wrong, Eddie. You know, if that was me, I mean, I'm just saying, if that was me, I'd call this guy up, and I would tear him a new one."

Eddie's steaming and says, "Yeah, yeah, that's right. That's what I'm gonna do." He goes flying down the hall back to his office and gets on the phone.

Earl follows him, walks in, draws his finger across his throat, and says, "You need to hang up."

But Eddie says, "What?"

Earl, laughing, says, "We got you again."

Hearkening back to Chapter 10, Realtors (or, Pigeons in The Park), it was established that Eddie had a dim view of realtors who mistreated him and his fellow loan officers. See the Lynn H. story. Earl, being new to The Company, was out soliciting business and happened to run into her, and when she saw that he was with The Company, she said, "Is Eddie still there?"

Earl thought, this was a great introduction; she knows The Company and their reputation. So, he tells her, "Yes, Eddie is still there."

Boom. That's not what she was thinking. It all went downhill from there.

As Earl was driving back to the office, all he could think was, what in God's name did Eddie do to this woman? When Earl mentioned to Eddie he ran into Lynn H., he got a similar outburst from Eddie.

Eddie foolishly asked, "Did she trash me?"

Earl, not wanting to listen to another ten-minute tirade, avoided providing a truthful answer.

Then there's the story about *White Gold* when Eddie was making the movie with the Pakistanis, and he was the movie star, absolute movie star. Being such a busy man, it was amazing that Eddie had the time to star in the blockbuster movie. The producers had to maintain a tight budget, so it was filmed out of a gas station in Falls Church, VA, and all they had to offer Eddie for payment was a chicken sandwich while he was on set. Take a look at the movie advertisement in Chapter 18, Saturday Night Live Mortgage, with the teaser headline: The

The BUGEATER LUNCH and SUPPER CLUB

Question Facing the World is *White Gold*. Maybe a better question is, why did they want Eddie in this movie?

And then there was the time Eddie took that $35,000 loss on the loan in Chapter 15, Mini-Marketeers and Pocket Locks. As previously noted, the Bugeaters were a very competitive group, and Eddie was not going to be outdone by Columbo.

One of the all-time favorite stories was when Earl came in for the interview at The Company with Mr. Z. How many times in the history of corporate America has an individual come in for an interview with a company executive and, when dropping the name of an employee he was friendly with, was told "Try another name."? See Chapter 2, The Bugeater Lunch and Supper Club.

Now it's time to focus on Bow the Clown Prince. The Bugeaters are in the office one day and Bow tells them he's going out to the Shenandoah Valley with Tim to go golfing. Golfing and, of course, a heavy dose of drinking. It happened to be a very busy time at The Company. Daddy had hired a bunch of temps to come in and make copies and do clerical work at the office.

Eddie and Earl went to Charli, who was processing for Bow at the time, and requested a borrower's name and phone number from one of Bow's files. They wrote up a script, and then selected one of the young temps to read it as a message into Bow's voice pager. They asked the young lady into Eddie's office and explained they wanted to make use of her acting talent. She must have been thinking, "I'm supposed to be here copying packages. What are these guys doing? They got me reading a script into a voice pager." Eddie and Earl had her do a few test readings, and after they were satisfied with her performance, they went live.

She recited, "Hello, Bow. This is Susan Jones. I'm sure you don't remember me. You took a loan application from me and my husband a week ago, and we have not heard anything from you or your staff. And if I don't hear from you by close of business tonight, we're going to take our loan elsewhere. Our phone number is 703-528-xxxx."

The plan worked perfectly.

Bow and Tim come off the golf course, drunk as a couple of monkeys, and go to Bow's car. Bow called into his pager and put it on speaker so Tim was a full witness to this as it happened. The second message broadcast was the one from Susan Jones. Bow freaked out when he heard the last of her message asking him to call her. He called Susan Jones, and she picked up.

She said, "Bow, I didn't call you."

Anybody with an ounce of common sense would have known the Bugeaters were gigging them, but not Bow, who's also severely inebriated.

So, he said, "Oh, my God, we gotta get your husband on the phone." So, he patches the husband in on a conference call. Bow tells the couple, "I think what we have here is a credit bureau conspiracy," which made no sense at all.

So, the couple is really freaking out because now the credit bureau is allegedly involved.

Bow goes home, passes out, then goes into the office the next day.

Earl is sitting in his office when Bow comes in. Bow was expecting to confront Earl about this bogus call and was prepared for him to offer up excuses as to why it couldn't have been him. But when Bow entered Earl's office, he just looked at Earl and said, "You did that, didn't you?"

And Earl said, "Yeah."

Bow didn't know what to say, so he just walked out. And then he put the word out that he wasn't going to talk to Eddie and Earl for two weeks. That was the best news those two had heard in a long time.

Bow's strategy of using "The Committee" as a completely fictitious entity to get more overage on his loans has been noted. Inasmuch as anything else, this antic contributed greatly to his winning of awards.

After reading these stories of the Bugeaters spoofing Bow, one would wonder, what on earth would compel him to turn his pager password over to them? To this day, that question remains unanswered.

Bow lived in a townhouse community. He had a small fenced-in backyard, and as he consumed his pizza and Chinese food, he would toss the empty boxes into the backyard. It got so bad that his HOA actually wrote him a letter telling him they would run him out of the community if he didn't clean up the trash. How did this letter get into the hands of the Bugeaters? Most certainly, Bow did not hand it to Earl or Eddie. It's just one of the many artifacts Earl collected over the years and wanted to write about someday.

When the Bugeaters came up with the Pontius Pilate award, Bow must've been the inspiration. For example, when customers would ask him pertinent questions, such as whether or not their loan was going to close on time, or if their loan was in underwriting, Bow would say he's just the loan officer, so how would he know such things? And just like Pilate, he would wash his hands of the matter and pass it off to someone else.

Whenever a customer was surprised at the settlement table with jacked-up points or interest rate, everyone sitting in the room would be calling Bow for an explanation. Finally, when the frustrated customer got on the phone, Bow just said, "Hey, I'm really glad you got your house." He hung up, and that was the end of that. He would sell a customer a loan product even though he had no idea how it worked. When asked, he didn't even try to provide an explanation. It was inconsequential to him. Just as when he scheduled three loan applications at the same time, jumping from one to the next, ticking off each customer, one after the other.

When Earl first thought about writing this book, it was partly to expose the many ridiculous aspects of this industry. For example, look no further than when this lady realtor had Bow writing an article for a real estate magazine, which was tantamount to a nun being asked to write a sex novel. All he did was plagiarize other articles. He had no idea what he was doing, but it made for good copy.

We talked about how Bow would make 400 rate sheets to take out on the street, but they would always end up in the dumpster instead. Why was he so gullible when Earl hit him up with the "Will work Easter Sunday" concept if he was just going to toss the sheets into the dumpster, anyway? Only Bow knows.

When Bow arrived at a real estate office, before he walked in, he would page himself. The timing was perfect. As he walked in the door, the pager would go off, and all the realtors could hear it. Then he'd ask if he could use a phone. He'd sit at a centrally located empty desk where everybody could hear him have a pretend conversation. "You're very welcome, Mr. Smith. I'm glad the settlement went well, and thank you for referring your brother to me, as well." Shame on those realtors who bought this bullshit but, apparently, many of them did.

Sean was a latecomer to the Bugeaters but started out with a bang. One October, Sean and his buddy decide that they're going to go up to West Virginia, which is an hour and a half away, to do some canoeing. The weather was beautiful with the fall foliage, 75 degrees, dry, a nice fall day. As they were driving, to enhance their experience, they decided to drop a couple of tabs of acid. They arrived at the river and rented a canoe. They get the canoe into the river and climb in, paddling away, looking around at all the foliage and scenery. They were so excited to be out on the water on such a beautiful day. Three hours later, they come down off the acid trip, and their canoe is still tied to the dock. There happened to be a father up in the parking lot with his eight-year-old son looking down at the scene. The son said, "Dad, what are those people doing down there?" And the father said, "Son, let me get back to you on that."

Sean had a refinance customer, a gentleman who worked for Janet Reno, the ex-Attorney General of the United States, and reported directly to her. Sean did a lot of business with a particular settlement officer, and the two of them planned to have the closing in the customer's office, which was on Capitol Hill. Both of them were supposed to go to the settlement, Sean and the settlement officer, but just before the appointed time, Sean calls up the settlement officer and says, "Hey, look, I'm not gonna be able to make this meeting today. And by the way, this guy isn't getting the interest rate he thinks he's gonna get. But you can handle it." Apparently, Sean played the market and lost. After being notified by the settlement officer that Sean was jerking him around, the customer went ballistic. He huffed and puffed and threatened to shut Sean and The Company down but finally capitulated and signed the paperwork. Sean was oblivious to the fact that this was not the customer to screw with.

There was another transaction involving the same settlement officer where Sean provided a construction loan for a house in Sean's neighborhood. Once again, Sean was supposed to be at the settlement but failed to show. The customer had many questions about the construction loan that the settlement officer was not equipped to answer. That was Sean's responsibility. The settlement officer was quite exasperated after the closing, and as he left the customer's house, Sean came riding up on a bicycle and asked, "Hey, how did the settlement go?" That was the way Sean did things; he was out riding a bike when he was supposed to be conducting business.

As previously noted, Tim was dangerous because he didn't know he was dangerous. Tim proved his mettle as an award winner due to the following accomplishments: Trying to take overage on a loan you can't take overage on, a state-funded loan program. After moving halfway across the country for a new job he knew nothing about, he spent the first day on the job at Camelot, a strip club, with Bow. A week later, when he had his first loan application scheduled, he blew it off to go to the strip club with Bow again. He became Bow's new valet, so that was a big strike against him. And then, after he got really tired of his brother, Johnny Gumba, berating him all the time, he would resign, re-date his resignation letter, and then change his mind and come back. We can't forget what an ass he made of himself on the Atlantic City trip by harassing the boat captain and Tim just being Tim. The difference between Tim and Bow was that Bow, to his credit, knew he was a joke. But Tim was dangerously oblivious to what a joke he was. If the Bugeaters had continued beyond 1995, Tim would have eclipsed everybody and dominated the awards.

The biggest upset in the history of the Bugeater awards was when Mookie stole Eddie's thunder as the primary contender for the first-year winner. Eddie had 14 out of 15 votes when Gumba came in and told the story about when Mookie told the couple on the phone that they had to get married in three days as one of the terms to qualify for the VHDA loan and then laughed about it. How could you not vote for that?

Just as Sean came in on the back side of the Bugeaters in the later days, The Zealist was in on the early days. One day, he is driving to the settlement to refinance his own house. He's on the beltway, and, of course, the traffic is bumper-to-bumper. Since he's a little behind, he calls the settlement office to say, "Hey, I am going to be ten minutes late, but don't worry, I'm coming."

The settlement officer responds, "Well, you don't really need to come."

The Zealist says, "Well, what do you mean? We're going to refinance."

The settlement officer said, "No, you're not."

The Zealist said, "What do you mean?"

And the guy at the settlement office tells him, "You just got fired."

The Company hadn't even told him.

Another time, The Zealist had some irate customers, which was not unusual for any of these characters. He was so distraught, thinking that this guy he pissed off was going to come looking for him, The Zealist and his wife moved out to Front Royal, Virginia, for the weekend, an hour and a half from The Company, going toward West Virginia. They holed up in a motel. It reminded Earl of the Clint Eastwood movie *The Outlaw Josey Wales*, where he had a bunch of people holed up in this cabin with the bad guys coming for him.

The Zealist overreacted, and it was a waste of time and money. The Zealist was known for holding court at Caldwell's, a bar on Little River Turnpike where there were so many mortgage companies that they called it Mortgage Banker Row. Most days at two o'clock, mortgage bankers would meet up at Caldwell's to drink and trade stories, trying to one-up each other. The Zealist was their top customer.

You can probably guess that the only two-time winner of the Mortgage Banker of the Year award was Bow the Clown Prince.

Acknowledgments

by Rick Soper

Having never written a book before and therefore an acknowledgment, it begs the question, "Where does one start, and where does one end?" In this case, the start is most obvious to me. Special thanks to Charlotte "Charli" Quinn and Chuck "Chairman" Cepak, without whose involvement and dedication this book does not exist. Charli is our agent and much, much more. Chairman is our financier and consultant. Thanks to my family, high school buddies, and frat house brothers who endured my sense of humor and obsession with pranking them and many others. I feel the book is an extension of those times. A neurologist who treated my wife Lisa during her long illness had a frame on his office wall that had many sayings and pieces of advice. One in particular stood out: "Every person should laugh at least once every day." I have always subscribed to that theory and always will.

And last but not least, to the Bugeaters, whose antics and overall hilarious approach to business and life made this book an easy and seamless endeavor. Of course, many thanks to our editor, Lynn Thompson, and our publisher, Becky Norwood, whose wealth of knowledge enabled us to bring this masterpiece to you, the reader, in an intelligible format. Lastly, our cover artist, Laura Ricci, deserves a standing ovation for bringing to life the vision that I have carried in my mind for many years for the cover of this book. She did an astounding job, true to my description.

Author Biographies

as told by their agent,
Charlotte Quinn
of Mighty Quinn Productions

Rick Soper – An Irish Italian born in Boston on St. Patrick's Day; Rick is true royalty. His passions run deep in rock 'n roll and sports. He watched the Celtics play at the Old Boston Garden as a kid. He was one of seven young men who received a scholarship to play basketball in Greece. His favorite rock 'n roll band is The Rolling Stones, and his knowledge of the band is encyclopedic. Rick was in the crowd of 600,000 in 1973 at the famous Summer Jam at Watkins Glen that featured The Allman Brothers Band, Grateful Dead, and The Band. These days, Rick is most likely to be found at the beach, vodka tonic in hand, or watching a vintage spaghetti western. Rick's loving and driven dedication to memorializing the unbelievable antics that occurred every day at The Company resulted in the book you are holding in your hands. For decades, he declared, "We gotta write a book someday!" With Rick's rich Boston accent and deep voice, we're looking forward to getting him lots of voice-over work.

Michael Gleeson – Mike was born and raised in O'Neill, Nebraska, the birthplace of the famous coach Frank Leahy. He was one of eight siblings. Their father was the mayor, so the unruly siblings were all untouchable. Mike carried this charm and has remained relatively unscathed throughout his wild and crazy life experiences. As a student, he was instrumental in getting his college to install a bar when he single-handedly procured funding from Coors and Schlitz. Mike ran it profitably for two years with wildly outrageous stories connected to this venture. He acquired his comedy skills from the great Bill Murray when he was classmates with Bill in college. While it's impossible to choose only a few highlights here, Mike has led a life full of hard-to-believe anecdotes, coincidences, and lofty acquaintances with the strange and unusual reputation of running into people he knows everywhere he goes. Everywhere. We are looking forward to publishing his next book that will tell the true tales of The Seven Degrees of Michael Gleeson. We can't wait to get started on it.

David Riddle – David was raised in Japan and California until his family relocated to the East Coast of the US. Golf, Guitar, and Grandkids rule David's world, not necessarily in that order. Just call him Triple G. He started golfing at 12 when his family lived in Okinawa. There was absolutely nothing else to do. He golfed every day after school for 50 cents. As a result, he played Varsity golf in high school and college after his family returned to the United States. David is successfully training his grandson, who recently caddied at the Arnold Palmer Invitational. When he isn't golfing or doting on his grandkids, David is channeling his inner Johnny Winter while playing his 2004 Firebird through his Princeton Chorus amp or his 1990 white Gibson Flying V. David is undoubtedly Johnny Winter's biggest fan and has become a talented blues guitar slinger in his own right. We're looking forward to booking David on a Johnny Winter tribute tour. Auditions for the band start soon.

www.ingramcontent.com/pod-product-compliance
Lightning Source LLC
Chambersburg PA
CBHW070549160426
43199CB00014B/2427